Ducasse
Made Simple
by Sophie

LES ÉDITIONS
Alain Ducasse

Acknowledgments

Bravo to Sophie Dudemaine for maintaining the spirit of my cooking in this book while making my dishes more accessible to the home cook. She chose and redefined my recipes with all the talent and insight one has come to expect from her.

Alain Ducasse

A warm and heartfelt thank you to Alain Ducasse, who had the generosity and trust to give me carte blanche in reworking these recipes. The project was an honor and a true pleasure.

My appreciation to chef Frédéric Vardon, liaison extraordinaire between the kitchens of Alain Ducasse and my own.

My gratitude to Emmanuel Jirou-Najou, Stéphanie Ruyer, and all the talented team at Les Éditions Alain Ducasse, and to Leslie Stoker and the staff at Stewart, Tabori & Chang; the expertise, patience, and hard work of all these people helped make this book a reality.

Thanks to Françoise Nicol and Catherine Madani for their splendid styling and photographs.

And kudos to my staff and faithful clientele at the Maison de Sophie for their enthusiastic participation while I was testing and sampling these recipes.

Sophie Dudemaine

I am very grateful to Holly Moore, wonderful cook, food stylist, and editor, who tested many of the recipes for the American edition of *Ducasse Made Simple by Sophie*.

I would also like to thank my friend and bon vivant Patrick Trautmann for his generous participation in the translation of this book. And a warm merci beaucoup to Alain Ducasse and Sophie Dudemaine for including me in this delicious project!

Linda Dannenberg

Ducasse
Made Simple
by Sophie

100 Recipes from the Master Chef
Simplified for the Home Cook
By **Alain Ducasse**
and **Sophie Dudemaine**

Recipes Adapted
by **Linda Dannenberg**

LES ÉDITIONS
Alain Ducasse

Contents

Introduction

Ducasse Made Simple by Sophie is a grand collaborative effort calling upon the talents of three key people on two continents. First and foremost is the extraordinary, world-renowned chef Alain Ducasse, whose score of restaurants in France and around the world have earned him more Michelin stars than any other chef in history. In every one of his restaurants Chef Ducasse is constantly refining and reimagining his cuisine. His dishes range from the rustic, soul-warming fare of the sublime Bastide de Moustiers in the hills of the Alpes-de-Haute-Provence to the rarefied and sophisticated dishes at Restaurant Alain Ducasse in Paris. The earthy Fillet of Cod with Savory White Beans and the Garden-Vegetable of Provence Slow Cooked in a Cast-Iron Pot are as representative of the Ducasse oeuvre as the Sautéed Foie Gras in Port Wine Sauce with Apples and Grapes or the Osetra Caviar with Chilled Langoustines in a Fragrant Bouillon, both exquisite choices from the Paris menu. The brilliance of Chef Ducasse's cuisine—lauded for its depth of flavor, exquisite and unique juxtapositions of ingredients, intriguing condiments and sauces, and elegance of preparation—has inspired joyful exclamations and superlative reviews across the globe. As the French magazine *Le Point* observed, "He is the Escoffier of our time."

Sophie Dudemaine, the author of 17 cookbooks and the star of a weekly cooking and entertaining show on French television, is the doyenne of French home cooking. In her books and on TV, Sophie's focus is on presenting easy-to-prepare recipes from widely available ingredients. She inherited her passion for cooking from a proud family tradition steeped in the worlds of cuisine, hotels, and entertaining. One grandfather was director of special events for the Eiffel Tower; her uncle is the celebrated chef André Daguin; other family members were hoteliers in the French provinces. She began her culinary career with apprenticeships at several of Paris' top restaurants: Faugeron, Apicius, and the Carré des Feuillants. She went on to become a caterer in and around Paris, with an exclusive clientele of small businesses and private Parisians. Between books and television engagements, she offers cooking classes and cozy country guestrooms at La Maison de Sophie, her bed-and-breakfast estate in Normandy near Deauville. Fascinated and dazzled by the cuisine of Alain Ducasse, Sophie initiated the idea for this book, proposing to produce her own adaptations of Chef Ducasse's recipes, specifically geared to the home cook. "In *Ducasse Made Simple by Sophie*," says Chef Ducasse, "Sophie has reinterpreted my recipes while respecting the spirit of every dish."

Alain Ducasse, Sophie Dudemaine

Linda Dannenberg, who produced the American edition of *Ducasse Made Simple by Sophie*, is the co-author, with Alain Ducasse, of *Ducasse: Flavors of France*, and the author of six cookbooks, including *Paris Bistro Cooking* and *Paris Boulangerie-Pâtisserie*. All the recipes in this volume have been retested in an American home kitchen using locally available ingredients. They remain true to the Ducasse originals, showcasing the imagination, the respect for ingredients, and the layers of texture and flavor that characterize every dish from this great chef. Dannenberg's brief introductions to each recipe incorporate Sophie's notes with her own insights and explanations about what makes each dish distinctive and what you need to know before proceeding with the recipe.

A Panoply of Recipes

The recipes presented here, selected by Sophie, offer a wide range of dishes from the Ducasse repertoire, from a simple, flavorful Cream of Pumpkin Soup or a Zucchini and Parmesan Risotto just right for a family supper, to a lush Lobster Newburg or Crispy Foie Gras Mousse Triangles perfect for an elegant dinner with friends. Vegetable dishes, including the Fricassee of Green Asparagus with Mushroom Ragout and Celery Root with Chestnuts, Chanterelles, and Shallots are as important and intriguing as the many recipes for fish, meats, and poultry. To crown the meal, there are many tantalizing dessert choices, among them Sauternes Fruit Gelée with Lemon Mousse and Lime Pound Cake; Caramelized Orange Tartlets; and Vanilla-Poached Rhubarb with Nectarine Compote and Red Berries, making the meal's finale a difficult decision. The recipes feature a variety of ingredients from lavish to humble, from foie gras and beef filet to pumpkin and potatoes, and intriguing, typically Ducassian combinations of elements, such as raw with cooked, or hot with cold. Several recipes showcase one element prepared three or four different ways—another Ducasse touch—such as a tomato appetizer, the Tomato Medley, with tomatoes marinated, baked, raw in a tartare, and stuffed; and a pear dessert, the Pear Medley: Three Variations on a Theme, composed of a pear clafoutis, a pear granité, and a pear compote.

At the back of the book is a selection of simple basic recipes that fall into one of two categories. There are fundamental recipes for components of other dishes featured in these pages, such as pastry

Sophie Dudemaine

Linda Dannenberg

doughs, tomato confit, garlic confit, chicken stock, and court bouillon. And there are also a handful of very simple, traditional recipes, such as those for tapenade, whipped cream, macaroni gratin, and tile cookies that are fine accompaniments not only to recipes in this book, but to many other dishes, and occasions, as well. Finally, at the end, you will find a source guide for specialized suppliers of many ingredients called for in these pages, as well as for cookware used in the recipes.

Preparation and Timing

Allowing ample time for the preparation of any dish makes cooking a greater pleasure. Time constraints and stress are often obvious in the final product. Note that several recipes in *Ducasse Made Simple by Sophie* involve elements that must be prepared a few hours, or even days, ahead of time. You should carefully plot out the timing for a dinner, giving yourself a broad window of time in which to prepare as much as possible before guests arrive.

A professional chef always precisely prepares and sets up all the ingredients he needs before beginning a recipe. Everything is prepared exactly as specified—chopped, minced, sliced, and measured—and then placed in a separate container, just like on a television cooking show where ingredients are displayed, ready to use, in little glass bowls. This is called the mise-en-place, literally "putting everything in place." Any recipe will be easier to accomplish, with the preparation flowing more smoothly, if you do your prep work the same way. Prepare your ingredients, line them up in the order that you'll need them, then assemble and lay out all the equipment you'll need for the recipe—bowls, whisks, knives, measuring spoons, spatulas, skillets, and so on. With this system, the recipe practically prepares itself!

Equipping and Stocking the Ducasse Home Kitchen

You don't need a professional array of kitchen equipment to create the recipes presented in this book, but you will certainly need a few basic items essential to the good home cook. These include a good food processor (a blender can often, but not always, stand in for a food processor); a sturdy electric mixer; a set of sharp knives; a large whisk and a small whisk; several skillets, including a cast-iron skillet, with lids; mixing bowls; a metal spatula; a large slotted spoon; individual (3- to 4-inch) and full-size (9- to 10 1/2-inch) tart pans with removable bottoms; a deep fryer (optional but helpful); a double-boiler; at least two food thermometers, such as on ovenproof metal dial thermometer and a candy and deep-fryer bulb thermometer, or instant-read digital thermometer; a grater, a zester, and a fine-mesh strainer; and Ball or Mason glass jars for storage. Three other kitchen items that are often called into service for Ducasse recipes may not yet be part of every home kitchen. One is a set of stainless steel pastry rings (these resemble tart pans, but with no bottom, just a simple metal circle), which come in a variety of sizes from 1 1/8 to 3 1/2 inches high and from 2 3/4 to 4 3/4 inches in diameter. These pastry rings are used to mold all kinds of dishes, from a stacked potato Mille-feuilles to a layered tart, into a perfect round form. The other items are a 6-cup nonstick silicone muffin mold, and a 15 by 12-inch nonstick silicone baking sheet. The silicone products are almost magical, heat resistant from -40°F up to 500°F, hygienic, easy to clean, and truly nonstick.

A few key ingredients make up the essential Ducasse pantry. These include a good fleur de sel, hand-harvested coarse-looking but delicate-textured sea salt from Brittany (Guérande or Noirmoutiers) or the Camargue region of France; high-quality extra-virgin olive oils, one rich, green and fruity for drizzling on a finished dish or salad, and a blander, paler oil for cooking; grapeseed oil, which has almost no flavor, good for frying without imposing a taste; canola, sunflower, or peanut oil for frying and sautéing; vinegars, especially a good sherry wine vinegar, a red wine vinegar, and a good, aged balsamic vinegar; a variety of good brine or oil-cured olives such as green Picholines, black Niçoise, brown-black Italian Gaetas, and purplish Greek Kalamatas. (Avoid American "canned ripe olives"; they look black but have no taste or character, having been processed first in an alkaline solution and then with an iron compound that turns green olives black.) Many recipes call for either Tomato Confit or Garlic Confit (see pages 186 and 187); it would be handy to prepare batches of both of these simple items and store them in glass jars to keep them always at the ready.

Bon Appétit!

First Courses:

Hors d'Oeuvres, Appetizers, and Soups

Chestnut Bouillon

Cream of White Bean Soup

Cream of Asparagus Soup

Cream of Broccoli Cappuccino Style with Ricotta Dumplings

Cream of Mussel Soup

Cream of Pumpkin Soup

Cream of Watercress Soup

Cream of Garlic Soup

Mushroom Omelette

Crispy Foie Gras Mousse Triangles

"Uncle John's" Fried Pumpkin Purses

A Tomato Medley

Cold Red Snapper Niçoise with Tomato Compote

Chicken Liver Terrine

Marinated Sea Scallop Salad

Tomato-Mozzarella Mille-feuilles

Salade à la Caesar

Salade Niçoise Monaco Style

Herbed-Duck Ravioli

[Bouillon de Châtaignes]

Chestnut Bouillon

Serves **6**

3 tablespoons unsalted butter

3 tablespoons extra-virgin olive oil

3 skinless, boneless chicken breast
halves (about 6 ounces each),
sliced into thin strips

3 shallots, sliced

6 garlic cloves, peeled and crushed

3 1/2 cups chestnuts, in a jar
or frozen

Fine sea salt

Freshly ground black pepper

1/2 cup cognac

4 cups chicken broth

2 cups heavy cream

1/2 cup heavy cream, whipped
to soft peaks

1/3 cup chervil sprigs or flat-leaf
parsley sprigs for garnish

This is a lovely fall soup—rich with the flavors of chestnuts, chicken, cognac, and cream—that would be an elegant first course for a Thanksgiving dinner.

In a large stockpot over medium-high heat, combine the butter with the olive oil and heat until the butter is melted and bubbling. Add the chicken and sauté, stirring frequently, until browned, about 10 minutes. Add the shallots, garlic, and chestnuts, stir to combine, then season with a pinch of salt and pepper. Reduce the heat to low, and cook for about 3 minutes, stirring occasionally. Add the cognac and stir well to combine. Add the chicken broth and 1 cup of the cream, and stir to combine. Bring to a boil over high heat, then reduce the heat to low and simmer for 40 minutes. Add the remaining 1 cup of cream, stir to combine, and cook for 20 minutes. Transfer the mixture to a food processor and purée until smooth, working in batches if necessary. Strain through a fine-mesh strainer into a saucepan and keep warm over medium-low heat. Taste and adjust the seasoning.

Pour the hot soup into warmed bowls and add a dollop of the whipped cream in the center of each bowl. Decorate with a few leaves of chervil and serve immediately.

[Soupe Glacée de Haricots Blancs]

Cream of White Bean Soup

Serves 6

1 pound dried white beans,
  such as Great Northern, picked
  over, rinsed, soaked overnight
  in water to cover, and drained*
4 to 5 cups chicken broth
1 cup light cream
1 rosemary branch
10 fresh sage leaves
Fine sea salt
Freshly ground black pepper
6 teaspoons extra-virgin olive oil
  for garnish

** Alternate soaking method: If you don't
have time to soak the beans overnight, try
this quick-soak method: Place the beans
in a medium casserole and cover with warm
water 2 inches above the surface of the
beans. Bring to a boil over high heat, cover,
remove from the heat, and let stand for 1 to
1 1/2 hours. The beans will swell to twice
their volume. Drain.*

Served hot or cold, this velvety soup with a Basque inspiration is versatile, easy and inexpensive to prepare, and richly satisfying. Remember to soak the beans the night before, or use the quick-soak method.

Combine the drained beans, chicken broth, cream, rosemary, 4 sage leaves, 1 teaspoon of salt, and a pinch of pepper in a large casserole and stir to combine. Bring to a boil over high heat, cover, reduce the heat to low, and cook, stirring occasionally, for 1 hour. Discard the rosemary and sage. Working in batches, transfer the soup to a food processor or blender and purée until smooth. If the purée is too thick, add 1/2 to 1 cup chicken broth and purée to blend. Taste and adjust the seasoning if necessary.

If serving cold, set the soup aside to cool, then refrigerate until ready to serve. If serving hot, return the soup to medium heat, bring to a simmer, and remove immediately from the heat.

Ladle the soup into bowls and drizzle each serving with 1 teaspoon of olive oil. Garnish each with a sage leaf and serve.

[Fine Crème d'Asperges]

Cream of Asparagus Soup

Serves **6**

For the soup

1/3 cup extra-virgin olive oil

3 pounds (approximately 3 bunches)
  green asparagus, trimmed,
  cut in 1/2-inch pieces

3 small new white onions,
  peeled and thinly sliced

1 teaspoon fine sea salt

Freshly ground black pepper

4 cups chicken broth

1/2 cup heavy cream

3 tablespoons chilled unsalted
  butter, cut into bits

For the garnish

One 7-ounce package of fresh chèvre
goat or sheep cheese

5 finely chopped fresh chives

1 tablespoon heavy cream

Fleur de sel, or coarse sea salt

Freshly ground black pepper

6 green asparagus, trimmed, peeled
  into thin strips with a vegetable
  slicer, and chilled

2 tablespoons olive oil

To prepare the soup

In a large stockpot, heat the olive oil over medium-high heat, add the asparagus pieces, onions, salt, and a few turns of freshly ground pepper, and stir to combine. Cook, stirring frequently, until the onions are soft and translucent, but not browned, and the asparagus turns bright green, 7 to 10 minutes. Add the chicken broth, stir to combine, and bring to a boil over high heat. Reduce the heat to low and simmer for 30 minutes, stirring occasionally. Carefully transfer the contents of the pot to a food processor or blender. Purée on high speed for 30 seconds. Add the cream and butter, and pulse for another 5 seconds. Return the mixture to the stockpot and keep warm over low heat.

To prepare the garnish and serve

In a medium mixing bowl, mash the cheese with a fork, and add the chives, cream, and a pinch of salt and pepper. Stir until smoothly blended. Pour the asparagus soup into six warmed bowls. Place a rounded tablespoon of the cheese mixture in the center of each bowl. Sprinkle with pepper. Drizzle the chilled asparagus strips with olive oil and sprinkle with a pinch of fleur de sel. Crown the center of each bowl with several asparagus strips. Serve immediately.

[Crème de Brocoli en Cappuccino]

Cream of Broccoli Cappuccino Style with Ricotta Dumplings

Serves **6** to **8**

For the soup

1 pound fresh or frozen broccoli
(6 to 7 cups), trimmed and
coarsely chopped
4 cups chicken broth
3/4 cup heavy cream
Fine sea salt
Freshly ground black pepper

For the dumplings

1 cup ricotta cheese
2 tablespoons all-purpose flour
2 large eggs
Fine sea salt
Freshly ground black pepper
1/4 pound Reggiano Parmesan
cheese, or other good Parmesan,
shaved into curls

This is a bright and easy-to-make soup enhanced by the addition of tangy little ricotta dumplings. As an easier variation, you can substitute dollops of slightly salted whipped cream for the dumplings: Combine 1/2 cup heavy cream and 1/4 teaspoon fine sea salt, and whip to firm peaks. Garnished with whipped cream, the soup really resembles its namesake cappuccino.

To prepare the soup

In a large stockpot, combine the broccoli, chicken broth, and heavy cream and bring to a boil over medium-high heat, stirring occasionally. Reduce the heat to low and simmer for 45 minutes, stirring occasionally. Working in batches, carefully transfer the soup to a food processor or blender, and purée until smooth and airy. Season to taste with salt and pepper, and purée another 5 seconds. Return the soup to the stockpot and keep warm over low heat.

To prepare the dumplings

Bring a large pot of water to boil. Fill a medium bowl with cold water and 4 or 5 ice cubes and set aside.

Combine the ricotta, flour, eggs, and a pinch of salt and pepper in a medium bowl, and whisk until blended. Using 2 teaspoons, shape the dough into little football-shaped dumplings and place directly into salted, simmering water; cover and cook for 3 minutes. Turn the dumplings over and cook 1 minute. Using a slotted spoon, transfer the dumplings to the bowl of ice water for about 15 seconds, then place on paper towels and very gently pat dry. Transfer the dumplings to an oiled bowl and set them aside until ready to serve.

Ladle the soup into warmed serving bowls and place 2 or 3 gnocchi in the middle of the soup. Sprinkle with Parmesan shavings and serve immediately.

[Crème de moules de Bouchot]

Cream of Mussel Soup

Serves **6**

4 to 5 pounds mussels,
   thoroughly cleaned and scrubbed
2 shallots, minced
1 onion, minced
4 cups dry white wine
1 bouquet garni (1 branch thyme,
   1 bay leaf, 3 strips orange zest,
   tied in a cheesecloth sachet)
Freshly ground black pepper
3 cups fish stock (or substitute
   1 1/2 cups chicken stock mixed
   with 1 1/2 cups clam juice)
1 tablespoon tomato purée
3 tablespoons cornstarch
1/8 teaspoon ground saffron
1 cup heavy cream
Fine sea salt

A classic, stocky French mussel soup, this dish often appears on menus as "Billi Bi" soup. Legend has it that it originated at Maxim's in Paris and was named after an American tin millionaire and regular patron named Billy B. Leeds. Cream, saffron, wine, and herbs give this soup its rich and savory flavor, while the generous garnish of whole mussels gives it texture and great visual appeal.

In a large stockpot, combine the mussels, shallots, onion, white wine, bouquet garni, and a few turns of freshly ground pepper. Cover the pot, bring the liquid to a boil over high heat, and cook until the mussels just open, about 7 minutes. Strain the mussels and reserve the liquid. Discard any unopened mussels. Remove the mussels from their shells and cover with some of the reserved cooking liquid until ready to use. Reserve 1/2 cup of mussels in a separate bowl to use as a thickener later on. Discard the shells.

Strain the remaining cooking liquid through a fine-mesh strainer. Combine the cooking liquid, mussels, and fish stock in a large stockpot and stir to combine. Place over high heat and bring to a rolling boil. Lower the heat to medium, and reduce by about half, approximately 30 minutes. In a small bowl, combine the tomato purée and cornstarch and whisk to blend. Add the tomato purée mixture to the cooking liquid and whisk to blend. Reduce the heat to medium-low and cook for 3 minutes. Add the heavy cream and saffron and cook for 3 minutes.

In batches, add the reserved 1/2 cup of mussels and cooking liquid to a food processor. Purée each batch until smooth, about 30 seconds, and return to the stockpot. Stir to blend the batches, then taste and adjust the seasoning if necessary. Ladle the soup into warmed soup bowls. Divide the remaining mussels among the soup bowls, arranging them around the edges of the bowl. Serve immediately.

[Crème de Potiron]

Cream of Pumpkin Soup

Serves **6**

2 tablespoons extra-virgin olive oil
1 onion, thinly sliced
1 leek (white part only), thinly sliced
1 pound sugar pumpkin, cut into
  small chunks and peeled
6 cups chicken broth
3/4 cup ricotta cheese
5 ounces slab bacon, diced small
1/2 cup heavy cream
Fine sea salt
Freshly ground black pepper

This is a lovely, bright fall soup. Look for a small (2- to 3-pound) "sugar" pumpkin that is ideal for cooking. (The large "jack-o'-lantern" pumpkins are too tough, and have lost their sugar; some have been wax-coated for longevity. Always make sure a pumpkin is suitable for cooking.) To dress this soup up in a variety of ways, Chef Ducasse suggests garnishes such as small, homemade croutons sautéed in butter, or a spoonful of wild mushrooms such as chanterelles, sautéed in olive oil. You could also add a pinch of spicy ground red chili pepper to the heavy cream before whipping.

In a medium stockpot, heat the olive oil over medium heat. Add the sliced onion and leek, and cook for 2 to 3 minutes, stirring frequently, until they soften and begin to look translucent. Stir in the pumpkin and a dash of salt and pepper. Add the chicken broth and bring to a boil over high heat. Reduce the heat to low and simmer for 45 minutes, stirring occasionally. Remove from the heat, add the ricotta cheese, and stir to combine. Transfer the mixture to a blender and purée until smooth. Adjust the seasoning to taste.

While the soup is cooking, heat a medium skillet over high heat. Add the bacon and cook, stirring frequently, until browned and slightly crispy. Set aside. In the bowl of an electric mixer, whip the heavy cream with a pinch of salt until the mixture forms stiff peaks.

Ladle the pumpkin soup into warmed bowls and garnish each serving with the diced bacon. Add a generous spoonful of whipped cream in the center of each bowl and serve immediately.

[Velouté de Cresson]

Cream of Watercress Soup

Serves **6**

8 tablespoons (1 stick)
   unsalted butter
One 10-ounce package frozen
   spinach, thawed
2 bunches watercress, washed, dried,
   thick stems removed
2 1/2 cups chicken broth
3/4 cup plus 2 tablespoons heavy
   cream
Fine sea salt
Freshly ground black pepper

This delicate yet richly flavored soup is quick to prepare and has a beautiful deep green hue. It requires just five minutes of prep time followed by twenty minutes of cooking. To make this soup more festive, garnish each serving with a few thin slices of broiled scallop, drizzled with olive oil and lemon juice. You can serve this soup warm or cold.

Heat the butter in a medium stockpot over medium-high heat until melted and just bubbling. Add the spinach and watercress and cook, stirring occasionally, until the leaves are fully wilted, about 5 minutes. Stir in the broth and 3/4 cup of cream. Bring the mixture to a light boil, reduce the heat to low, and simmer, uncovered, for 15 minutes, stirring occasionally.

Working in batches, carefully transfer the hot soup to a food processor or a blender, and purée until smooth. Season with salt and pepper, pulse to blend, then return the soup to the stockpot and heat to a simmer. Ladle the soup into warmed bowls, drizzle with a few drops of the remaining 2 tablespoons of cream to decorate, and serve immediately.

[Crème d'Ail]

Cream of Garlic Soup

Serves **6**

2 tablespoons extra-virgin olive oil

2 ounces slab bacon, diced small

1 medium onion, thinly sliced

3 cups rich chicken broth

8 garlic cloves, halved, germ (green sprout in the center) removed

2 russet potatoes, cut into chunks

1 bouquet garni (1 branch thyme and 1 bay leaf, tied in a cheese-cloth sachet)

Fine sea salt

Freshly ground black pepper

Fleur de sel, or coarse sea salt

2 tablespoons chopped flat-leaf parsley

This flavorful, creamy soup is actually made without any cream at all. The smooth, velvety texture comes from a purée of the broth with potatoes, onion, garlic, and other ingredients.

If you can find it, pink garlic (known in France as ail rose de Lautrec) substituted for the everyday white-skinned variety makes this soup even more intense. In France, this soup is often garnished with a raw egg yolk in the center, but if you have health concerns about eating raw eggs, it's better to serve it without the yolk. For another tasty garnish, slice two garlic cloves very thin, ideally with a mandoline, and sauté them in olive oil until they are crispy and golden. Scatter these crunchy garlic chips over the top of the soup just before serving.

In a medium stockpot, heat the olive oil over medium heat, then add the bacon and onions and sauté, stirring frequently, for about 3 minutes, until the bacon is lightly browned and the onions begin to turn translucent. Add the chicken broth and bring to a boil. Add the garlic, potatoes, bouquet garni, and a pinch of salt and pepper and stir to combine. Cover, reduce the heat to medium-low, and simmer, stirring occasionally, for 40 minutes.

Transfer the soup to a food processor or blender and purée until smooth and creamy. Pour into heated bowls, garnish with a sprinkle of chopped parsley and a pinch of fleur de sel, and serve immediately.

[Champignons en Omelette]

Mushroom Omelette

Serves 6

1 1/2 pounds white mushrooms, cleaned, caps and stems separated
Juice of 1 lemon
11 tablespoons unsalted butter
3 shallots, minced
2 garlic cloves, peeled and chopped
Fine sea salt
Freshly ground black pepper
3/4 cup beef stock
2 tablespoons heavy cream
Freshly ground black pepper
12 large eggs
4 teaspoons extra-virgin olive oil
8 fresh chives

Here is a classic French omelette with an unusual and delicious mushroom filling composed of both creamy puréed mushrooms and sliced sautéed mushrooms. The four omelettes have to be prepared separately, so at serving time you have a decision to make: Serve each one as soon as it's prepared, or keep the finished omelettes warm in a low oven until all are ready to serve at once. Serve with a green salad dressed with a tangy vinaigrette and crusty country bread.

Preheat the oven to 200°F. Slice the mushroom caps and sprinkle with lemon juice. In a large skillet, melt 4 tablespoons of the butter over high heat, add the sliced mushroom caps, and stir to coat with the butter. Sauté for 1 minute without stirring, then sauté 3 to 4 minutes, stirring frequently, until the mushrooms start to release their liquid. Add two-thirds of the shallots and garlic, sprinkle with salt and pepper, stir to combine, and cook for 1 minute. Add 1/2 cup of the beef stock, stir to combine, reduce the heat to low, and simmer, stirring occasionally, for 15 minutes. Transfer to an ovenproof bowl and keep warm in the oven.

Mince the reserved mushroom stems. In the skillet, melt 3 tablespoons of the butter over high heat, then add the minced stems to the skillet and stir to coat well with the butter. Sauté for 1 minute without stirring, then cook 2 to 3 minutes, stirring occasionally, until the mushrooms begin to release their liquid. Add the remaining one-third of the shallots, sprinkle with salt and pepper, and cook, stirring occasionally, for 3 minutes. Transfer the mushroom mixture to a food processor and purée. Return the mixture to the pan over medium heat, add the remaining 1/4 cup of beef stock, and stir to combine. Reduce the heat to low and simmer for 5 minutes. Add the cream, season to taste, and stir to combine. Transfer the mixture to a separate ovenproof bowl (not the bowl with the mushroom caps) and keep warm in the oven.

Break the eggs into a large bowl, sprinkle with salt and pepper, and whisk until frothy. In an omelette pan or an 8-inch skillet, combine 1 teaspoon of the olive oil and 1 tablespoon of the butter over medium-high heat. When the butter is melted and bubbling, pour in one-fourth of the egg mixture and cook the omelette, lifting the edges around the omelette with a spatula, and tipping the pan slightly so that uncooked egg runs to the bottom. Cook until the center is soft and just cooked through. Spread one-fourth of the mushroom purée over the lower half of the omelette. On top of the purée, layer on one-fourth of the sliced mushroom-cap mixture, then fold the top half over the bottom half of the omelette and transfer to a serving plate. Keep warm in the oven. Repeat with the remaining 3 omelettes. Garnish each omelette with two chives and serve immediately.

[Rissoles Croustillantes de Foie Gras]

Crispy Foie Gras Mousse Triangles

Makes 30 triangles; serves 6 as an appetizer

Twelve 17 by 12-inch phyllo sheets,
  thawed if frozen
3/4 pound store-bought foie gras
  mousse, such as D'Artagnan;
  or substitute good goose
  or pork pâté
Fleur de sel, or coarse sea salt
1/4 cup extra-virgin olive oil

A great hors d'oeuvre that will disappear in a flash, these crispy mouthfuls with meltingly good foie gras in the center are easy to prepare from store-bought ingredients. They also make an appealing first course accompanied by a salad of bitter greens, such as arugula, radichio, and endive. Phyllo pastry, which wraps the foie gras mousse, can be a little tricky to work with since the sheets are so fragile and dry out quickly. Thaw the phyllo exactly according to package directions, then keep all but the sheets you're working with under slightly damp paper towels covered by plastic wrap.

Preheat the oven to 350°F. Place 2 stacked phyllo sheets horizontally (long edge toward you) onto a clean work surface and cut lengthwise into four 17 by 3-inch strips. Place 1 tablespoon of foie gras mousse at one end of the first strip about 1 inch in from the edge, sprinkle with fleur de sel, then fold the corner over to make a small triangle. Continue folding the strip back and forth in successive triangles, as you would a flag, until it forms a neat triangular packet. Moisten the remaining edge with a bit of water on your fingertips and press gently to close. Repeat with the remaining 3 strips of phyllo, then lay out 2 new sheets of phyllo and repeat the process. Continue 4 more times, until you have created 24 triangles.

Place the triangles on a greased baking sheet, lightly brush them with olive oil, and bake in the center of the oven for 5 to 7 minutes, until the dough turns golden brown. Serve on a platter as an hors d'œuvre, or divide among six individual plates and serve with a green salad as a first course.

[Barbajuans d'Hiver]

"Uncle John's" Fried Pumpkin Purses

Makes 15 purses

1/2 pound peeled and diced sugar
   pumpkin, or butternut squash,
   peeled and diced
3 garlic cloves, crushed
7 tablespoons extra-virgin olive oil
1 leek (white part only), sliced
1/2 cup cooked Arborio rice,
   or other short-grain rice
1 tablespoon grated Reggiano
   Parmesan, or other good Parmesan
   cheese
1 large egg, beaten
Fine sea salt
Freshly ground black pepper
1 recipe "Uncle John" Olive Oil
   Pastry Dough (see page 191),
   or 1/2 pound refrigerated
   commercial pizza dough
About 6 cups peanut oil,
   or other vegetable oil, for frying
Fleur de sel, or coarse sea salt

These small, plump pastry purses, filled with pumpkin, rice, leeks, and Parmesan cheese are called "Uncle John's"—Barba Juan—in the dialect of Monaco. Golden and crispy they are a terrific hors d'oeuvre to serve with a white-wine-and-cassis kir or other aperitif. You can prepare the purses and refrigerate them up to three hours ahead of frying and serving.

To prepare the filling

Preheat the oven to 300°F. In a 13 by 9-inch or other large baking dish, combine the pumpkin, garlic, and 3 tablespoons of the olive oil. Bake in the center of the oven, uncovered, for 1 hour, stirring occasionally. Meanwhile, heat a small skillet over medium heat. Add 2 tablespoons of the olive oil and the leek slices and sauté, stirring occasionally, until soft, translucent, and slightly browned, about 5 minutes. Set aside.

In a large bowl, combine the pumpkin, leek, rice, Parmesan, egg, and the remaining 2 tablespoons of olive oil. Season with salt and pepper and set aside.

To assemble and cook the purses

On a floured work surface, using a floured rolling pin, roll out the pastry dough to a 1/4-inch-thick rectangle. Using a 2- to 2 1/2-inch cookie or biscuit cutter, cut out 30 circles. Place 1 to 2 tablespoons of filling in the center of 15 of the pastry rounds. Moisten the edges of the rounds with water and top with the remaining 15 pastry rounds. Seal the edges by crimping with a fork or pinching with your fingers. Heat the oil to 325°F in a large, deep, heavy-bottomed pot and fry the purses, 6 to 8 at a time, until puffed and golden brown, 3 to 4 minutes. Turn them over once during the cooking time. Using a slotted spoon, transfer the purses to a baking sheet lined with a double layer of paper towels to drain. Sprinkle with fleur de sel and serve immediately.

[Méli-Mélo de Tomates]

A Tomato Medley

Serves **6**

For the marinated tomatoes

8 plum tomatoes, peeled, quartered,
    and seeded
3 branches basil, leaves picked,
    stems removed
2 garlic cloves, peeled and chopped
4 tablespoons extra-virgin olive oil
1/2 teaspoon fine sea salt
1 teaspoon confectioners' sugar

For the baked tomatoes

One 15-ounce can tomato purée
24 pieces Tomato Confit (see
    page 186), or sun-dried tomatoes in
    oil, drained
4 tablespoons heavy cream
1/4 cup grated Reggiano Parmesan
    cheese, or other good Parmesan
Fine sea salt
Freshly ground black pepper

For the tomato tartare

8 ripe plum tomatoes, peeled, diced,
    and seeded
1 shallot, minced
5 fresh basil leaves, chopped
2 tablespoons balsamic vinegar
Fine sea salt
Freshly ground black pepper

For the almond-stuffed tomatoes

6 plum tomatoes
1 cup almonds, minced
18 fresh basil leaves, chopped
2 tablespoons extra-virgin olive oil
1 tablespoon balsamic vinegar
Fine sea salt
Freshly ground black pepper

1/2 cup chopped fresh basil leaves
    for garnish

You create four separate small recipes to achieve this striking dish. Prep time is about one hour, cooking time about one hour and forty-five minutes, so plan accordingly. You can prepare the baked marinated tomatoes a day ahead to the point where you sprinkle them with Parmesan, and set aside. Cover the gratin dish with aluminum foil and refrigerate until ready to broil and serve.

To prepare the marinated tomatoes

Preheat the oven to 250°F. In a large gratin dish, mix the tomatoes, basil, garlic, and olive oil and sprinkle with salt and sugar. Cover with aluminum foil and bake for 1 1/2 hours. Set aside.

To prepare the baked tomatoes

In a medium skillet, reduce the tomato purée over medium-high heat until the liquid has evaporated, 5 to 7 minutes. Season with salt and pepper, then pour over the marinated tomatoes (recipe above). Arrange the pieces of tomato confit over the marinated tomatoes. Drizzle with the cream, sprinkle with the Parmesan cheese, and set aside.

To prepare the tomato tartare

Place the diced tomatoes in a strainer set over a plate, sprinkle with salt, and set aside for 10 minutes; this helps the tomatoes release some of their water. (You can use the tomato water for a tasty Tomato Vinaigrette; see page 189.) Combine the tomatoes, shallots, basil, and vinegar in a medium bowl. Sprinkle with a pinch of salt and pepper, stir to combine, and set aside.

To prepare the almond-stuffed tomatoes

Cut a 1/2-inch slice from the top of each tomato, creating a "lid." Scoop out the seeds and membranes from the interior of the tomatoes, being careful not to cut through the outer skin. Sprinkle the interiors with salt, place the tomatoes upside down on a wire rack set over a large plate, and allow them to drain for 15 minutes.

Meanwhile, combine the almonds, the 18 chopped basil leaves, oil, and vinegar in a medium bowl. Fill the tomatoes with the mixture and set aside.

To serve

Preheat the broiler. Spoon the tomato tartare into six clear juice glasses and set aside. Place the baked tomatoes under a broiler for 3 minutes, until the top is bubbling and slightly browned. Divide the baked tomatoes among six dinner plates, placing them along one side of each plate. Set the glasses of tomato tartare next to the baked tomatoes, and arrange the almond-stuffed tomatoes in the space remaining. Sprinkle with the 1/2 cup of chopped basil and serve.

[Rougets Froid à la Niçoise]

Cold Red Snapper Niçoise with Tomato Compote

Serves **6**

For the tomato compote

2 tablespoons extra-virgin olive oil
1 tablespoon sugar
2 pinches dried oregano
Two 15-ounce cans whole peeled
  tomatoes, drained, quartered,
  and seeded
3/4 cup fish stock (or substitute
  1/2 cup chicken stock mixed with
  1/4 cup clam juice)
Fine sea salt
Freshly ground black pepper
1/2 bunch basil, stems removed,
  leaves chopped

For the red snapper

2 tablespoons extra-virgin olive oil,
  plus more for garnish
12 red snapper fillets
  (about 3 ounces each)
18 brine-cured or oil-cured small
  black olives, such as Niçoise
Fresh basil leaves for garnish
Fine sea salt

Perfect for a summer lunch or a generous appetizer at dinner, this dish features quickly sautéed fish fillets accompanied by a thick tomato compote savory with herbs. The recipe, which has its origins in Nice, originally called for the Mediterranean fish rougets, or red mullet, which is difficult to find in the United States. The fish featured here is the more accessible red snapper.

To prepare the **tomato compote**

Combine the olive oil, sugar, oregano, and tomatoes in a large skillet over medium-high heat. Reduce, stirring occasionally, until all of the liquid has evaporated, about 5 minutes. Add the fish stock, stir to combine, and cook until all the liquid evaporates and the mixture is very thick, about 5 minutes more. Add the basil, season to taste with salt and pepper, and set aside to cool to room temperature.

To prepare the **red snapper**

Heat the olive oil in a large skillet over high heat. Add the fillets, skin side down, and cook for 2 minutes. Turn and cook on the opposite side for 30 seconds more. Set aside to cool.

To serve

Divide the tomato compote among six serving plates. Place 2 red snapper fillets on top of each serving and drizzle with olive oil. Scatter a few of the black olives over the fish and sprinkle with basil leaves. Season with a pinch of sea salt and serve.

[Terrine de Foies de Volaille]

Chicken Liver Terrine

Serves 6 to 8

For the brandy mixture

1/4 cup cognac
2 tablespoons port
2 tablespoons sherry

For the chicken livers

1/2 pound chicken livers, trimmed
  and halved
1/4 cup brandy mixture (see above)
1 garlic clove, chopped
1 teaspoon fine sea salt
1/2 teaspoon freshly ground
  black pepper
1 tablespoon chopped fresh thyme
1 tablespoon minced flat-leaf parsley
1/2 teaspoon ground allspice

For the terrine lining (barding fat)

1/2 pound bacon, thinly sliced
3 1/2 tablespoons brandy mixture
  (see above)
1/2 teaspoon ground allspice
1 tablespoon chopped fresh thyme

For the stuffing

1/2 pound ground pork
1/2 pound chicken livers, trimmed
  and halved
1/2 teaspoon ground allspice
1/2 tablespoon brandy mixture
  (see above)
2 small branches thyme
1 teaspoon fine sea salt
1/2 teaspoon freshly ground
  black pepper

This is a rustic, robust terrine from the heart of the French countryside, the perfect first course for a long, lazy Sunday afternoon dinner with family and friends. Serve with crisp, toasted slices of baguette, cornichons—the tiny, tangy French pickles—some strong Dijon mustard, and a sturdy, tannic red wine. You can also accompany the terrine with chunky onion marmalade or confit. Note: This dish must be prepared forty-eight hours in advance.

To prepare the brandy mixture

Combine all the ingredients in a small bowl and set aside.

To prepare the chicken livers

Combine all the ingredients for the chicken livers in a medium bowl, stir to mix well, cover, and marinate in the refrigerator for 2 hours.

To prepare the terrine lining

Combine all the ingredients for the terrine lining in a medium bowl, stir to coat the bacon slices, cover, and marinate in the refrigerator for 2 hours.

To prepare the stuffing

Combine all the ingredients for the stuffing in the bowl of a food processor and pulse until smoothly blended. Cover and refrigerate until ready to use.

Preheat the oven to 275°F. Line the bottom and sides a loaf pan with overlapping slices of the bacon, letting the excess drape over the sides of the pan. Spread half of the stuffing mixture in the bottom of the pan and top with a layer of the chicken livers. Repeat with the remaining stuffing mixture and chicken liver mixture. Fold the excess bacon strips over the top of the terrine. Place a piece of aluminum foil slightly larger than the pan directly on top of the bacon, pressing down gently to release any air pockets trapped in the terrine, then tucking the foil ends in around the terrine to seal. Place the loaf pan in a 13 by 11-inch baking dish or roasting pan and fill with water to halfway up the side of the loaf pan. Bake for 1 1/2 hours, or until an instant-read thermometer registers 160°F. Remove to a wire rack to cool, then refrigerate in the pan for 48 hours before serving.

Cut into 1/2-inch-thick slices with a small, sharp knife. You have the choice of removing the bacon lining, or leaving the slices intact. Serve with baguette toasts.

[Noix de Saint-Jacques en Salade]

Marinated Sea Scallop Salad

Serves **6**

For the salad

6 medium new potatoes
36 pieces Tomato Confit
  (see page 186), or sun-dried
  tomatoes in oil, drained
1 shallot, chopped
1 teaspoon chopped fresh thyme
9 tablespoons extra-virgin olive oil
One 16-ounce bag baby spinach
  leaves
1 tablespoon sherry vinegar
Fine sea salt
Freshly ground black pepper

For the sea-scallop topping

18 medium sea scallops, thinly sliced
2 cups fresh lemon juice

This light and flavorful salad features seviche-style scallops that are marinated in lemon juice but are essentially raw. Always use very fresh scallops. If you prefer not to eat raw shellfish, you can sear the scallops for a minute on each side in a small amount of olive oil before proceeding with the recipe. Begin preparations about 2 hours ahead of serving. If you wish, you can garnish each serving with a few delicate shavings of Reggiano Parmesan cheese.

To prepare the salad

Combine the potatoes in a large saucepan with enough water to cover by 2 inches, and bring to a boil over medium-high heat. Cook for 20 minutes, until soft. Drain the potatoes, cool slightly, and peel them while still warm. Cut them into 1/4-inch slices. Combine the potato slices, tomatoes, shallots, and thyme leaves in a large bowl. Drizzle with 6 tablespoons of the olive oil, sprinkle with salt and pepper, and gently stir to combine. Cover with plastic wrap and marinate for 1 hour in the refrigerator.

Meanwhile, prepare the vinaigrette: Combine the sherry vinegar and 1/4 teaspoon salt in a small bowl and whisk to dissolve the salt. Add the remaining 3 tablespoons of olive oil, season with pepper, and whisk to blend. Set aside until ready to use.

To prepare the sea scallops

Combine the scallop slices and lemon juice in a bowl. Cover with plastic wrap and marinate in the refrigerator for 30 to 40 minutes.

To serve

Divide the spinach among six serving plates and arrange one-sixth of the potato slices atop each serving in an overlapping circle. Scatter 6 pieces of tomato confit over the potatoes, and drizzle with a teaspoon or two of the some of the olive oil–thyme marinade. Divide the scallop slices among the servings, arranging them in the center of each plate like the petals on a flower. Season with salt and pepper, drizzle with the vinaigrette, and serve immediately.

[Mille-feuilles de Tomate Mozzarella]

Tomato-Mozzarella Mille-feuilles

Serves **6**

This is an attractive and unusual presentation for a tomato and mozzarella appetizer, an imaginative variation on a theme. To make each mozzarella slice perfectly uniform, you can trim the edges with a 2 1/2- to 3-inch cookie cutter. Choose garden-fresh or vine-ripened tomatoes, if possible.

For the mille-feuilles

1/4 cup balsamic vinegar
Fine sea salt
1/2 cup extra-virgin olive oil
Freshly ground black pepper
6 large garden-fresh or vine-ripened
  tomatoes, each cut horizontally
  into 4 even slices, seeded
  (slice a sliver off the bottom slices
  to help the mille-feuilles stand
  upright)
Two 1-pound rounds fresh
  mozzarella (buffalo if possible),
  each cut into nine 1/4-inch-thick
  slices
3 small red onions, thinly sliced
1/2 bunch basil, stems removed,
  leaves coarsely chopped
Fleur de sel, or coarse sea salt,
  optional

For the salad garnish

1 tablespoon red wine vinegar
Fine sea salt
2 tablespoons extra-virgin olive oil
Freshly ground black pepper
1/3 pound mesclun salad greens

To prepare the mille-feuilles

Combine the vinegar and a pinch of salt in a small bowl and whisk to dissolve the salt. Add the olive oil and a pinch of pepper and whisk to blend. Set aside. On each of six serving plates, stack the bottom slice of one tomato, a slice of mozzarella, and a slice of onion, then sprinkle with a teaspoon of chopped basil. Repeat two more times with the tomato, mozzarella, and basil layers, then crown with the top slice of the tomato, stem still attached if possible. Drizzle with 2 tablespoons of the vinaigrette and, if you wish, a pinch of fleur de sel.

To prepare the salad garnish

Combine the vinegar and sea salt in a medium bowl and whisk to dissolve the salt. Add the olive oil and a pinch of pepper and whisk to blend. Add the mesclun and toss to coat the greens with the dressing. Divide the salad among the serving plates, arranging it around each mille-feuilles, and serve.

[Sucrines à la Caesar]

Salade à la Caesar

Serves 6

For the Caesar dressing

2 large egg yolks
1 tablespoon Dijon mustard
Juice of 1 lemon
1 garlic clove, minced
1 cup extra-virgin olive oil
1/2 cup grated Reggiano Parmesan
   cheese, or other good Parmesan
1 anchovy fillet, minced
1 tablespoon chopped fresh tarragon
Freshly ground black pepper

For the salad

1 long, very thin baguette, sliced
   in half lengthwise, each half cut
   into thirds
1 garlic clove, peeled and halved
6 small butterhead lettuces,
   leaves torn into large pieces
12 slices smoked bacon, cooked
   until crisp
1 lemon, zest, pith, and skin
   removed, sliced into segments,
   seeded
1/4-pound chunk Reggiano Parmesan
   cheese, or other good Parmesan,
   shaved into thin curls with
   a vegetable peeler

Dressed up with bacon, tarragon, diced lemon, and garlic-rubbed baguettes, this is a Caesar Salad extraordinaire. There are, of course, the traditional Parmesan cheese, anchovies, and garlic as well, but instead of the typical romaine lettuce, this recipe calls for the smaller and more tender butterhead lettuce. If you prefer not to use raw egg yolk in the dressing, you can substitute 2 tablespoons of real mayonnaise for the yolks. For a more substantial appetizer, top each serving with a handful of grilled shrimp.

To prepare the Caesar dressing

Combine the egg yolks, mustard, lemon juice, and garlic in a large mixing bowl, and whisk until smoothly blended. Let sit for 5 minutes to thicken. Add the olive oil in a slow, steady stream, whisking vigorously until completely incorporated. Add the Parmesan, anchovy, and tarragon, and stir to combine. Season to taste with salt and pepper and set aside.

To prepare the salad

Preheat the broiler. Rub the baguette slices with the cut sides of the garlic clove. Toast the slices under the broiler until well browned. Combine the lettuce and the Caesar dressing in a salad bowl and toss gently to coat the lettuce. Divide among six salad plates and top each with 2 slices of bacon, the toasted baguette slices, and the lemon segments. Sprinkle with the Reggiano Parmesan shavings and serve.

[Salade Niçoise à la Monegasque]

Salade Niçoise Monaco Style

Serves **6**

For the vinaigrette
Juice of 2 lemons
Fine sea salt
1/2 cup extra-virgin olive oil
Freshly ground black pepper

For the tapenade garnish
12 thin slices of long,
   narrow baguette, toasted
1 garlic clove, peeled and halved
1/3 pound Provençal Olive Paste
   (see page 189)
3 tablespoons extra-virgin olive oil

For the salad
1 celery stalk, cut into 2-inch pieces
One 6-ounce jar roasted red bell
   peppers, cut into strips
1 cup fava or baby lima beans,
   shelled if fresh, or thawed if frozen;
   marinated 1 hour or more
   in extra-virgin olive oil to cover
6 small spring onions, or pearl
   onions, peeled and thinly sliced
5 frozen or canned artichoke hearts,
   thawed or drained, thinly sliced
6 plum tomatoes, peeled, quartered,
   and seeded
4 radishes, thinly sliced
1 cucumber, peeled and diced
1/2 pound mesclun salad
Two 6-ounce cans light tuna fillets
   in oil, drained
24 small black Niçoise olives,
   or other small black olives,
   such as Kalamata
1/2 bunch basil, stems discarded,
   leaves coarsely chopped
Fine sea salt
Freshly ground black pepper

To prepare the vinaigrette

Combine the lemon juice and a generous pinch of salt in a medium mixing bowl and whisk to dissolve the salt. Add the olive oil and a pinch of pepper and whisk to blend. Set aside.

To prepare the tapenade garnish

Rub 1 side of the toasted baguette slices with the cut surfaces of the garlic clove, then spread each with a thin layer of the tapenade. Add the olive oil to the remaining tapenade and stir to incorporate. Transfer to a small crock or serving bowl and set aside.

To serve

In a large bowl, toss the celery, bell peppers, fava beans, pearl onions, artichokes, tomatoes, radishes, and cucumber. Divide the mesclun among six serving plates and top with the vegetable mixture. Garnish with the tuna fillets and the black olives, dividing them equally among the six servings. Drizzle with the vinaigrette, and sprinkle with salt, pepper, and basil. Place 2 tapenade toasts on each plate and serve, accompanied by the crock of the tapenade mixture to pass at the table.

[Ravioli de Canard]

Herbed-Duck Ravioli

Makes approximately 48 raviolis; serves 12 as an appetizer, 6 as a main course

Using wonton wrappers is an easy and practical way to make tender and tasty ravioli. These are stuffed with a flavorful combination of duck breast and fresh herbs, and drizzled with a buttery reduction sauce.

For the herb stuffing

1 tablespoon extra-virgin olive oil
10 ounces mesclun salad mix
2 tablespoons chicken stock
1/3 cup coarsely chopped fresh
   chervil or cilantro
1/3 cup coarsely chopped fresh
   chives
1 teaspoon chopped fresh oregano
   or marjoram, or 1/2 teaspoon dried

For the duck stuffing

2 boneless magret duck breasts
   (7 to 8 ounces each), skin on
6 tablespoons extra-virgin olive oil
1 medium white onion, minced
1 garlic clove, peeled and crushed
1 1/2 cups chicken stock
1 teaspoon balsamic vinegar
Fine sea salt
Freshly ground black pepper

For the ravioli

One 12-ounce package wonton
   wrappers
3 tablespoons unsalted butter,
   chilled and cut into bits
Fine sea salt
Freshly ground black pepper
6 to 12 sprigs chervil or curly
   parsley, optional for garnish

To prepare the **herb and duck stuffing**

Heat the olive oil in a large skillet over medium heat. Add the mesclun and chicken stock and stir to combine. Cover and cook until wilted, about 4 minutes, stirring occasionally. Remove from the heat and add the chervil, chives, and oregano, stir to combine, and set aside.

Cut three small slits into the fatty skin of each duck breast, taking care not to cut through to the meat. Set aside. Heat 4 tablespoons of the oil in a large skillet over high heat. Place the breasts, skin side down, into the skillet, reduce the heat to medium, and cook for 5 minutes. Add the minced onion and garlic and cook for 3 minutes, stirring occasionally to keep the garlic and onions from burning. Add the chicken stock, reduce the heat to low, cover and simmer for 20 minutes.

Transfer the duck breasts to a cutting board, and remove the skin and fat. Cut the breasts into large chunks, then place them in a large bowl and set aside. Strain the cooking liquid through a fine-mesh strainer into a saucepan and reserve. Remove the garlic from the strainer, and add the remaining onions to the duck. Add the reserved herb and mesclun mixture to the duck and onion mixture and stir well with a wooden spoon to combine. Working in batches, place the duck mixture into a food processor and pulse until the mixture is finely chopped. Transfer the duck mixture to a large bowl. Add the balsamic vinegar and the remaining 2 tablespoons of olive oil, season with salt and pepper, and mix well with a wooden spoon to combine. Set aside.

To prepare the **ravioli**

Open the stack of wonton wrappers and cover with a slightly damp towel until you're ready to use them; this prevents them from drying out as you work. Place a rounded tablespoon of the stuffing in the center of each wonton wrapper. Fold the dough in half to obtain a triangle. Seal the edges with a bit of water and press the dough together, then fold 2 corners in toward the center, leaving 1 pointed corner on top. Set aside, covered with plastic wrap, until ready to cook.

To serve

Bring a large pot of salted water to boil. Meanwhile, bring the reserved duck cooking liquid to a boil over high heat, lower the heat to medium, and reduce by half, about 10 minutes. Whisk in the butter, a little at a time, until blended, and set the sauce aside. Add the ravioli to the boiling water and cook just until soft, 1 to 2 minutes. Divide the ravioli among six warmed soup bowls or pasta dishes (or among twelve bowls if serving as a first course), spoon the sauce over them, sprinkle with salt and pepper, garnish with a sprig of chervil or parsley, if you wish, and serve warm.

Fish

Baked Sea Scallops with Beef Sauce

Lobster Newburg

Fillet of Sole in the Style of "Riche"

Thick-cut Salmon Fillets with Morel Mushrooms

Thick-cut Salmon Fillets with Tomato Sauce

Fillet of Sole with Shrimp Stuffing

Almond-Crusted Fillet of Sole

Provençal-Style John Dory with Slow-Cooked Zucchini

Vegetable Tartlets with Roasted Prawns

Double-Breaded Oysters with Fresh Tartar Sauce

Half-Salted Cod with White Beans

Sea Bass in Herb Butter with Chanterelles

Hake with Pine Nut Chutney

Bay of Biscay Tuna Fillet

Shrimp Darioles

Anchovy Tart

[Noix de Saint-Jacques en Daube]

Baked Sea Scallops with Beef Sauce

Serves **6**

This unusual dish, in which you prepare a beef stew whose strained sauce serves to garnish the grilled sea scallops, is actually a two-meals-in-one recipe. You have the scallops in beef sauce for dinner one night, and the remaining beef stew the next, served with buttered noodles, or chopped up as part of a traditional shepherd's pie. Serve the scallops with braised Belgian endives or rice.

For the citrus butter

3 tablespoons unsalted butter,
  softened
Zest of 1 orange
Freshly ground black pepper

For the beef stew

3 cups dry red wine
4 tablespoons extra-virgin olive oil
2 pounds beef stew meat
  (chuck or round or a combination
  of the two), cut into 1-inch cubes
2 carrots, peeled and diced
2 onions, peeled and diced
2 oranges, peeled, segments
  separated, and seeds removed
3 cups veal or chicken stock
1 branch thyme
8 whole, unpeeled garlic cloves
1 bay leaf
10 whole black peppercorns
One 15-ounce can tomato purée
2 tablespoons chopped fresh basil

18 large sea scallops
Zest of 1 orange

To prepare the citrus butter

Combine the butter, zest, and a sprinkle of pepper in a small bowl and stir well to blend. Store in the refrigerator until ready to use.

To prepare the stew

Preheat the oven to 250°F. Pour the red wine into a large saucepan and bring to a boil over high heat. As soon as the wine reaches a boil, carefully bring a lighted match or barbecue lighter to just above the surface of the wine and flambé, not touching the pot until the flames die out. Remove from the heat and set aside.

Heat the olive oil in a large ovenproof pot over medium-high heat. Add the beef and cook, turning often, until browned. Add the carrots, onions, and orange segments, stir to combine, and continue to cook for 2 minutes. Raise the heat to high, add the reserved wine, and reduce for 5 minutes. Add the veal stock, garlic cloves, thyme, bay leaf, and peppercorns and stir to combine. Cover, place in the center of the oven, and bake for 3 hours.

With a slotted spoon, transfer the beef, vegetables, and oranges to a large bowl, leaving as much sauce as possible in the pot. Reserve the beef mixture in the refrigerator for another use. Strain the remaining sauce through a fine-mesh strainer into a saucepan. Add the tomato purée, stir to blend, and reduce over high heat, stirring occasionally, until the sauce thickens, approximately 30 minutes. Remove from the heat, add the basil, and let infuse for 3 minutes. Strain the sauce through a fine-mesh strainer into a saucepan and set aside.

To finish and serve

Preheat the oven to 450°F. In a large nonstick sauté pan over high heat, sear the scallops until golden brown on both sides, no more than 1 minute per side. Place the scallops on a baking sheet and top each scallop with a dab of the citrus butter. Place in the center of the oven and cook for 3 minutes, until the butter melts and the scallops are just cooked through. Meanwhile, reheat the reserved sauce over medium heat. Divide the scallops among six warmed serving plates. Pour melted citrus butter from the baking pan into the warming sauce and whisk to blend. Spoon the sauce generously around the scallops, garnish the scallops with orange zest, and serve immediately, accompanied by braised endive or buttered rice.

[Homard Breton Newburg]

Lobster Newburg

Serves **6**

For the lobster

2 quarts Court Bouillon
 (see page 188)
6 live female lobsters (approximately
 1 1/2 pounds each)

For the coral butter

10 fresh basil leaves, thinly sliced
8 tablespoons (1 stick) unsalted
 butter, softened
Coral (roe) and green tomalley (liver)
 from the lobster

For the Newburg sauce

4 tablespoons extra-virgin olive oil
4 tablespoons unsalted butter
6 lobster heads (reserved, directions
 follow)
2 garlic cloves, peeled and coarsely
 chopped
2 shallots, peeled and coarsely
 chopped
6 tomatoes, coarsely chopped
1 fennel bulb, coarsely chopped
2 tablespoons tomato purée
3/4 cup sherry
2 cups fish stock (or substitute
 1 cup chicken stock mixed
 with 1 cup clam juice)
1 branch basil
Coral butter (reserved, above)
1 tablespoon heavy cream
Fine sea salt
Freshly ground black pepper

Lobster for six is always a splurge, but this Newburg dish would be a great treat for an elegant dinner. The sauce, a real enhancement to the sweet, tender lobster, is rich and flavorful, with depth from the sherry and savor from the fennel, shallots, and garlic. Serve with steamed basmati rice.

To prepare the lobsters

Bring the court bouillon (aromatic stock) to a boil in a large stockpot or lobster pot over high heat. Add the lobsters and steam for 17 minutes, covered. Remove the lobsters with a skimmer and set aside to cool. Separate the heads and tails, and set the tails aside. Cut the heads in half vertically, pull the head sac out and remove the intestines. Remove and reserve the green tomalley. Cut the halves of the head in half again, this time horizontally, and reserve. Remove the flesh from the claws and the tails from the shells, preferably in one piece. Cover and reserve the meat.

To prepare the coral butter

In a small bowl, combine the basil, butter, coral and green tomalley and mix to a smooth paste. Cover with plastic wrap and reserve in the refrigerator.

To prepare the Newburg sauce

In a large stockpot, combine the oil and butter and heat over medium-high heat until the butter is melted and bubbling. Add the reserved lobster heads and cook, stirring frequently, for about 3 minutes. Add the garlic, shallots, tomatoes, and fennel and stir to combine. Cook, stirring occasionally, for 3 minutes, until the vegetables start to soften. Add the tomato purée and sherry, stir to combine, and cook until the liquid reduces by half and thickens slightly, about 7 minutes. Add the fish stock and the branch of basil and stir to combine. Reduce the heat to medium-low and simmer, uncovered, for 40 minutes.

In a food processor or blender, purée the sauce, then strain it through a fine-mesh strainer into a large saucepan; discard the solids. Over high heat, reduce the strained sauce by half, 7 to 8 minutes. Add the cream and the reserved coral butter, whisk to blend, and adjust the seasoning to taste.

To finish and serve

Add the reserved lobster tails to the sauce, stir to combine, and simmer on low heat for 3 to 5 minutes, or until the lobster is heated through. Add the claw meat and any remaining lobster meat and stir to combine. Slice the lobster tails into 4 or 5 pieces. On each of six warmed serving plates, arrange 1 tail and 2 claws, then drizzle with the Newburg sauce. Serve immediately, accompanied by basmati rice.

Fish

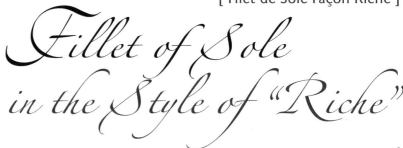
Fillet of Sole in the Style of "Riche"

Serves **6**

The Café Riche was a famous nineteenth-century Paris restaurant celebrated for its fillets of sole bathed in velvety cream sauces and garnished with lavish ingredients such as lobster and truffles. This fillet of sole recipe, which includes a buttery bread-crumb topping for the baked sole, is a contemporary homage to the old Riche. Here the fillets are surrounded by a rich mushroom cream sauce and garnished with garlicky prawns.

For the mushroom cream sauce

2 tablespoons extra-virgin olive oil
4 shallots, chopped
2 lemons, sliced
1 pound cremini mushrooms,
  stems trimmed, sliced
3/4 cup heavy cream
Fine sea salt
Freshly ground black pepper
4 tablespoons unsalted butter,
  chilled and cut into bits

For the herbed bread crumbs

6 tablespoons unsalted butter
1/2 cup plain fresh bread crumbs
3 tablespoons chopped mixed herbs
  (choose 2 or 3 among chervil,
  parsley, cilantro, and tarragon)
Fine sea salt
Freshly ground black pepper

For the prawns

2 tablespoons extra-virgin olive oil
1 garlic clove, chopped
24 large prawns, or jumbo shrimp
2 tablespoons flat-leaf parsley,
  minced
Fine sea salt

For the sole

12 sole fillets (3 to 4 ounces each)
Fine sea salt
Freshly ground black pepper
4 tablespoons unsalted butter

To prepare the mushroom cream sauce

Warm the olive oil in a large skillet over medium-high heat. Add the shallots, lemon, and mushrooms and stir to combine. Reduce the heat to medium, cover, and cook for 5 minutes without stirring. Uncover, add the cream, and stir to incorporate. Raise the heat to high and reduce the mixture, stirring frequently, for 5 minutes. Strain the sauce through a fine-mesh strainer, pressing on the mushrooms to extract their juice, and return to the saucepan over medium heat. Discard the solids. Season the sauce to taste with salt and pepper. Whisk in the butter, a little at a time, until incorporated. Transfer to a bowl, cover with aluminum foil, and keep warm in a low oven.

To prepare the herbed bread crumbs

Melt the butter in a large skillet over medium-high heat. Add the bread crumbs and toss to coat with the butter. Remove from the heat, add the herbs, and stir to combine. Season with salt and pepper and set aside.

To prepare the prawns

Heat the olive oil in a skillet over medium-high heat. Add the garlic and prawns and sauté for 2 minutes, stirring frequently. Remove from the heat, stir in the parsley, and season with salt. Keep warm in a low oven.

To prepare the sole and serve

Preheat the oven to 475°F. Season the sole with salt and pepper and arrange in a single layer on a baking sheet. Spread each fillet with a layer of the herbed bread crumbs and top each with 1 teaspoon of butter. Bake in the center of the oven for 6 to 7 minutes, until the fish is flaky. Spoon the cream of mushroom sauce onto six warmed serving plates. Top each serving with 2 sole fillets, garnish with 3 prawns, and serve immediately.

[Pavé de Saumon aux Morilles]

Thick-cut Salmon Fillets with Morel Mushrooms

Serves **6**

The thick-cut salmon fillet is the succulent star in this recipe, superbly accompanied by morel mushrooms and thyme-flavored, sautéed potatoes. The recipe calls for dried morels, but if you have the opportunity to use fresh ones, all the better! Be sure to clean the mushrooms carefully, since even a little bit of sand or grit can ruin the dish. Also, take the time to clarify the butter so the potatoes don't burn.

For the garnish

1/2 pound dried morels
   or 1 1/4 pounds fresh morels
4 tablespoons unsalted butter
1 garlic clove, peeled and crushed
1/2 cup beef stock
2 shallots, minced
Juice of 1/2 lemon
Fine sea salt

For the potatoes

1 pound (4 sticks) unsalted butter,
   clarified (see page 188)
24 small fingerling or tiny
   new potatoes, peeled
1 small branch thyme
1/2 teaspoon fleur de sel,
   or coarse sea salt

For the salmon

3 tablespoons unsalted butter plus
   1 tablespoon for finishing
1 tablespoon extra-virgin olive oil
6 thick-cut salmon fillets
   (about 6 ounces each)
Fleur de sel, or coarse sea salt
Freshly ground black pepper

To prepare the garnish

If using dried morels, rehydrate the mushrooms by soaking them in 3 cups of just-boiled water off the heat for 1 hour. Transfer with a slotted spoon to a strainer to drain. Reserve the liquid, if you wish, for sauces or other uses. If using fresh morels, cut off the stem of the mushrooms, then clean them several times in cool water, swishing them around to remove sand and grit lodged in the tiny nooks and crannies. Strain and dry them well.

In a large skillet, melt the butter over medium-high heat, then add the rehydrated or cleaned, fresh morels, garlic, and a pinch of salt, and stir to combine. Cook on low heat, stirring frequently, for 1 minute. Cover and cook for 10 minutes more, stirring occasionally, until their juice is extracted. Reduce the heat to low, add the beef stock, and simmer for 15 minutes. Remove the morels with a strainer and set aside. Reserve the liquid.

To prepare the potatoes

In a medium stockpot over medium heat, combine the clarified butter with the potatoes, thyme, and fleur de sel. Cook, stirring often, until the potatoes are soft, about 20 to 25 minutes. Set aside in the pot.

To prepare the salmon

In a large skillet, combine the 3 tablespoons of butter and the oil over medium heat and cook until the butter is melted and bubbly. Sprinkle both sides of the salmon steak with salt and pepper. Cook for 3 minutes on each side. Transfer to a warm platter and keep warm in a low oven.

To finish and serve

In a large skillet, melt the remaining 1 tablespoon of butter. Add the shallots, morels, and lemon juice and stir to combine. Cook for 2 minutes, stirring occasionally, until the shallots soften. Add the reserved morel liquid and simmer for 3 minutes. Season with salt and pepper to taste. Place a salmon fillet in the center of each of six heated serving plates. Divide the morels and the potatoes among the plates, spooning the morels along one side of the salmon and the potatoes along the other side. Sprinkle with fleur de sel and freshly ground pepper, and serve immediately.

[Pavé de Saumon aux Tomates Confites]

Thick-cut Salmon Fillets with Tomato Sauce

Serves **6**

For the sauce

One 15-ounce can tomato purée
Fine sea salt
Freshly ground black pepper
1 cup chicken stock
3 tablespoons balsamic vinegar
4 tablespoons unsalted butter,
  chilled and cut into small bits
1/2 bunch basil leaves,
  stems discarded, leaves coarsely
  chopped

For the salmon

18 pieces Tomato Confit
  (see page 186), or sun-dried
  tomatoes in oil, drained
3 tablespoons unsalted butter
1 tablespoon extra-virgin olive oil
Coarse sea salt
6 center-cut salmon fillets
  (5 to 6 ounces each)
10 basil leaves, coarsely chopped

Salmon and tomatoes are delightful partners in this quick-and-easy dish. The mild acidity of the tomatoes is a pleasing counterpoint to the richness of the fish.

To prepare the sauce

Reduce the tomato purée in a medium skillet over high heat, stirring frequently, until most of the liquid has evaporated, about 5 minutes. Season with salt and pepper, and add the chicken stock, stirring to combine. Cook, stirring occasionally, until the mixture reduces by half, about 10 minutes. Add the balsamic vinegar and stir to blend. Whisk in the butter, a little at a time, until incorporated. Add the basil leaves, season to taste with salt and pepper, and keep warm over very low heat.

To prepare the salmon

Preheat the oven to 300°F. Spread the tomato confit segments in a single layer on a small baking sheet, then place in the center of the oven and warm for 10 minutes; turn off heat but keep warm in oven until ready to serve. Warm the butter and oil in a large skillet over medium-high heat until butter is melted and frothy. Add the salmon steaks and cook for 3 minutes per side for medium. Sprinkle the steaks with coarse sea salt, transfer to warmed serving plates, and garnish each with 3 pieces of tomato confit. Ladle the tomato sauce around the fillets (or serve the sauce separately in a sauceboat), sprinkle with the chopped basil, and serve.

[Filet de Sole Tartiné de Crevettes]

Fillet of Sole with Shrimp Stuffing

Serves **6**

For the shrimp stuffing

30 small shrimp, peeled and
  deveined
2 shallots, halved
1/4 pound mushrooms,
  stems removed for the sauce,
  caps quartered
1 cup walnuts
10 coarsely chopped fresh chives
2 tablespoons extra-virgin olive oil
Fine sea salt
Freshly ground black pepper

For the sauce

2 tablespoons extra-virgin olive oil
1 onion, minced
1 carrot, thinly sliced
Reserved mushroom stems
  from stuffing, chopped
Fine sea salt
Freshly ground black pepper
1/2 cup dry white wine
2 cups chicken stock
3 tablespoons unsalted butter,
  cut into bits

For the sole

6 sole fillets (6 to 7 ounces each),
  cut lengthwise into thirds
Fine sea salt
Freshly ground black pepper
2 tablespoons unsalted butter plus
  butter for the dish
18 steamed medium shrimp, peeled
2 tablespoons chopped fresh chives
  for garnish

In this sole recipe, a delicious stuffing of shrimp, shallots, mushroom, and walnuts enhances the delicate flavor of the fish, and adds another element of texture. To simplify this dish, leave the six fillets whole rather than slicing them in thirds, lay them flat in the baking dish, and spread the stuffing over the top of each fillet. Bake as directed.

To prepare the shrimp stuffing

Combine the shrimp, shallots, mushroom caps, walnuts, chives, and olive oil in the bowl of a food processor and pulse until finely chopped. Season with salt and pepper and refrigerate until ready to use.

To prepare the sauce

Heat the olive oil in a large skillet over medium-high heat. Add the onion, carrot, and reserved mushroom stems, season with salt and pepper, and cook for 3 minutes, stirring frequently, until the onions and mushrooms soften. Add the wine, cook for 2 minutes, then add the chicken stock and stir to combine. Reduce the heat to medium low and simmer, stirring occasionally, for 30 minutes. Strain the sauce, then reduce over high heat until about 3/4 cup remains and the sauce has slightly thickened, 8 to 10 minutes. Remove from the heat and whisk in the butter, a little at a time, until combined. Season to taste with salt and pepper. Keep warm over very low heat.

To prepare the sole

Preheat the oven to 475°F. Season the sole with salt and pepper, then spread the stuffing evenly over the fillets. Roll the fillets over the stuffing jelly-roll style and secure with a toothpick. Place the fillets in a buttered baking dish. Place in the center of the oven and bake for 6 minutes.

Meanwhile, in a medium skillet, melt the butter over medium-high heat, and sauté the steamed shrimp until warmed through, about 1 minute. Season with salt and pepper. Carefully remove the fillets from the baking dish, and divide among six warmed serving plates. Garnish each with 3 steamed shrimp, spoon the sauce around the fillets, sprinkle with the chives, and serve.

[Solette Dite "Langue d'Avocat"]

Almond-Crusted Fillet of Sole

Serves **6**

6 large egg yolks
Fine sea salt
Freshly ground black pepper
2 cups sliced almonds, finely ground
6 sole fillets (6 ounces each),
  cut lengthwise into thirds
6 tablespoons unsalted butter
2 lemons, cut into wedges,
  for garnish
2 tablespoons chopped flat-leaf
  parsley for garnish

Here's an easy-to-prepare fillet of sole with a crispy, crunchy almond crust that will please everyone in the family, especially the kids. Instead of a single fillet flat on the plate, these fillets are cut in long strips for eye appeal and maximum crunch. Serve with steamed potatoes.

Whisk the egg yolks in a medium bowl until blended and season with salt and pepper. Spread the ground almonds on a dinner plate. Dip the sole pieces one at a time into the egg mixture, and then into the ground almonds, coating thoroughly. Set them on a baking sheet covered with parchment paper. Sprinkle the coated fillets with salt and pepper.

Melt 4 tablespoons of the butter in a large skillet over medium heat. Working in batches, sauté the sole until golden brown, approximately 2 minutes per side. Transfer the batches to a warmed platter, and keep warm in a low oven. Remove any burned bits and crumbs from the skillet with a spatula, then add the remaining 2 tablespoons of butter and melt over medium heat. Drizzle the melted butter over the sole fillets and sprinkle with parsley. Garnish the platter with lemon wedges, and serve, accompanied by steamed potatoes.

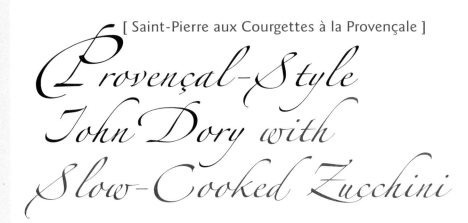

[Saint-Pierre aux Courgettes à la Provençale]

Provençal-Style John Dory with Slow-Cooked Zucchini

Serves 6

For the diced zucchini

4 tablespoons extra-virgin olive oil
6 small zucchini, diced
2 garlic cloves, peeled and crushed
1 sprig thyme
Fine sea salt
Freshly ground black pepper
2 basil leaves, sliced in fine julienne

For the John Dory

3 1/2 cups chicken stock
8 John Dory fillets (about 3 ounces
  each) (if you can't find John Dory,
  substitute pompano or sole)
2 lemons, sliced
3 plum tomatoes, sliced
1 fennel bulb, outer layers and fronds
  removed, minced
Fine sea salt
Freshly ground black pepper
1/2 cup extra-virgin olive oil
1 tablespoon fennel seeds
1 branch basil, stem removed, leaves
  coarsely chopped
18 pitted black olives, sliced
Fleur de sel, or coarse sea salt

The flavors of southern Provence and France's Mediterranean coast—a mélange of lemons, tomatoes, fennel, garlic, and olives—highlight this savory recipe for firm, fine-textured John Dory. If you can't find John Dory (sometimes called St. Peter's Fish), use pompano or sole instead. The zucchini slow-cooks in olive oil to tender perfection. Serve with whipped potatoes or Eggplant Caviar (page 189).

To prepare the diced zucchini

Heat 2 tablespoons of the olive oil in a large skillet over medium heat. Add the zucchini, garlic, and thyme, and stir to combine. Reduce the heat to low, cover, and cook, stirring occasionally, until the zucchini is soft, about 40 minutes. Remove and discard the thyme sprig and garlic clove, add the remaining 2 tablespoons olive oil, season with salt and pepper, and stir gently to combine. Sprinkle with the julienne of basil and keep warm in a low oven.

To prepare the John Dory

Preheat the oven to 425°F. Reduce the chicken stock by half in a large saucepan over high heat; set aside. Arrange the fish fillets in a large casserole dish, scatter the lemons, tomatoes, and fennel around the fish, and season with salt and pepper. Drizzle with the olive oil and the reduced chicken stock, then scatter on the fennel seed and chopped basil. Bake in the center of the oven for 20 minutes, basting with the pan juices halfway through.

To serve

Carefully transfer the fillets to a platter and keep warm in a low oven. Strain the pan juices through a fine-mesh strainer into a saucepan and reserve the solids. Place the saucepan over medium-high heat and reduce the juices, stirring occasionally, until the sauce is slightly thickened, about 10 minutes. Divide the reserved diced zucchini among 4 warmed serving plates. Place 2 fillets on top of each serving and drizzle with the sauce. Garnish with the reserved cooked slices of lemon, tomatoes, and fennel. Scatter on the black olives, sprinkle with a pinch of fleur de sel and a little pepper and serve immediately.

For the tartlet shells

1 recipe Flaky Short-Crust Dough (see page 191), or one 15-ounce package prepared pie crust dough, such as Pillsbury Rolled Refrigerated Pie Crusts

For the prawn sauce

4 tablespoons extra-virgin olive oil
Prawn or shrimp heads (reserved from prawns in prawn garnish, below)
1 shallot, minced
2 plum tomatoes, sliced
Fine sea salt
Freshly ground black pepper
2 tablespoon dry white wine
2 cups fish stock (or substitute 1 1/2 cups chicken stock mixed with 1/2 cup clam juice)
1 bunch basil

For the vegetable filling

3 tablespoons extra-virgin olive oil
6 fresh or frozen asparagus, bottoms trimmed off 4 inches from the tips; cut into 1/4-inch pieces
3 baby carrots, peeled and cut into 1/4-inch slices
3 baby or small turnips, peeled, cut in half and thinly sliced into half-moons
3 frozen or canned baby artichoke hearts, thawed or drained, thinly sliced
12 pearl onions, peeled and thinly sliced
12 pieces Tomato Confit (see page 186), or sun-dried tomatoes, cut into thin strips
6 small radishes, root ends and tops trimmed off, thinly sliced
Fine sea salt
Freshly ground black pepper
1/2 cup chicken stock

For the prawn garnish

2 tablespoons extra-virgin olive oil
1 tablespoon unsalted butter
18 large prawns or jumbo shrimp, peeled, heads reserved for prawn sauce (above)
Fine sea salt
Freshly ground black pepper
10 leaves fresh basil, chopped

[Langoustines Rôties et Tartelettes aux Légumes]

Vegetable Tartlets with Roasted Prawns

Serves **6**

The tartlet shells in this bright and elegant dish hold a bounty of mixed vegetables topped by succulent prawns. The eight vegetables that the recipe calls for are a bit labor-intensive to prepare, but the results won't disappoint. Serve these tartlets as a light lunch, or as a hearty appetizer.

To prepare the tartlet shells

Preheat the oven to 350°F. On a floured work surface, using a floured rolling pin, roll out the dough to a 1/8-inch-thick rectangle (or, if using store-bought pastry dough, roll out into two 1/8-inch-thick circles). Using a 5-inch biscuit cutter or an inverted 5-inch bowl as a guide, cut six 5-inch circles from the pastry dough. Press the dough gently into the bottoms and sides of six buttered, 4-inch, removable-bottom tart molds, then prick the bottoms of the crusts several times with the tines of a fork. Line the shells with aluminum foil or parchment paper, then fill to the brim with baking weights or dried beans. Place on a baking sheet and bake in the center of the oven for 8 minutes. Remove the baking weights and the foil, return to the oven, and bake for 10 to 12 minutes, until the crusts are golden brown. Transfer the tartlets, still on the baking sheet, to a wire rack to cool.

To prepare the prawn sauce

Heat the olive oil in a large saucepan over medium-high heat. Add the prawn heads, shallot, and tomato and stir to combine. Season with salt and pepper. Raise the heat to high and sauté for 3 minutes, stirring frequently. Add the white wine and fish stock, reduce the heat to medium low, and simmer for 45 minutes, stirring occasionally. Add the basil and simmer 10 minutes more. Strain the sauce through a fine-mesh strainer into a bowl, then return the strained liquid to the saucepan. Reduce the sauce by half over high heat, stirring occasionally. Taste and adjust the seasoning if necessary, and set aside.

To prepare the vegetable filling

Warm the olive oil in a large pot over medium-high heat. Add the asparagus, carrots, turnips, artichokes, onions, tomatoes, and radishes, and stir to combine. Season with salt and pepper. Sauté for 10 minutes, stirring frequently, then add the chicken stock and simmer for 5 minutes, stirring occasionally. Set aside in a low oven until ready to use.

To prepare the prawn garnish and serve

Combine the oil and butter in a medium skillet over high heat, stirring until the butter melts. Add the prawns and sauté 2 to 3 minutes, stirring frequently, until they are cooked through. Divide the vegetables among the six tartlet shells and arrange 3 prawns on top of each serving. Drizzle with the reserved sauce, sprinkle with salt, pepper, and chopped basil, and serve.

[Huîtres Panées]

Double-Breaded Oysters with Fresh Tartar Sauce

Serves **6**

For the tartar sauce

I cup mayonnaise

2 tablespoons minced herbs
(choose 2 among parsley, chervil,
chives, and tarragon)

2 cornichons (French sour gherkins),
chopped

I tablespoon capers

I small white onion, finely chopped

Fine sea salt

Freshly ground black pepper

For the sauce Villeroi

2 tablespoons truffle oil, or unsalted
butter, softened

2 tablespoons all-purpose flour

1/4 cup heavy cream

1/4 cup chicken stock

Reserved oyster liquid
(approximately 3/4 cup) (see below)

For the oysters

30 oysters, shucked, liquid reserved

2 large eggs

I teaspoon extra-virgin olive oil

I teaspoon soy sauce

Fine sea salt

Freshly ground black pepper

2 cups unseasoned dried bread
crumbs

1/4 cup all-purpose flour

Grapeseed or vegetable oil for frying

Cayenne pepper, optional for garnish

2 tablespoons chopped parsley,
optional for garnish

Crisp on the outside, delectably tender on the inside, these twice-breaded oysters are a briny treat. The oysters are accompanied by an herbed, fresh tartar sauce, which you can serve in a well-washed oyster shell, as shown in the photograph, right. (The photo also shows a shell holding the Villeroi sauce, used to coat the oysters before breading). You will need a large, deep, heavy-bottomed pot, and a deep-fry thermometer, important for getting the temperature of the oil just right.

To prepare the tartar sauce

Combine all of the ingredients for the sauce in a small bowl and season to taste with salt and pepper. Cover with plastic wrap and refrigerate until ready to serve.

To prepare the sauce Villeroi

Warm the truffle oil in a medium skillet over medium-high heat. Add the flour a little at a time, whisking continuously to blend. Cook for I to 2 minutes, whisking continuously. Add the cream, chicken stock, and reserved oyster liquid and continue to whisk until the sauce thickens, about 2 minutes. Set aside to cool to lukewarm.

To prepare the oysters

Combine the oysters and the Villeroi sauce in a large bowl and stir with a wooden spoon to coat the oysters well. Arrange the oysters on a small baking sheet or a platter that will fit in your freezer. Spread any sauce remaining in the bowl over the oysters. Lay a sheet of plastic wrap directly on top of the oysters, then place them in the freezer for 30 minutes. Meanwhile, combine the eggs, olive oil, and soy sauce in a medium bowl and whisk to blend. Season with a pinch of salt and pepper. Place the bread crumbs on one plate, and the flour on another. Remove the plastic wrap from the oysters and coat each in the flour. Dip the oysters a second time into the egg mixture and then into the bread crumbs, creating a double-thick coating. Place on a baking sheet lined with parchment paper or aluminum foil and set aside.

To fry and serve

Fill a deep (at least 8 inches high), heavy-bottomed pot with 4 inches of the oil and heat to 365°F, which is very hot but not smoking. Working in batches, add the oysters one-third to one-half at a time and fry, turning once or twice, until golden brown, approximately 3 minutes. Drain the fried oysters on paper towels and keep warm in a low oven until ready to serve. Arrange 5 oysters on each serving plate and garnish with a dollop of tartar sauce. Sprinkle with salt, black pepper, cayenne, and parsley if you wish. Serve immediately.

[Cabillaud Demi-Sel Meunière]

Half-Salted Cod with White Beans

Serves **6**

2 pounds kosher salt

I cup sugar

4 skinless cod fillets
   (6 to 7 ounces each)

Freshly ground black pepper

I pound dried white beans,
   such as Great Northern, picked over,
   rinsed, soaked overnight in water
   to cover, and drained*

Fine sea salt

4 fresh sage leaves

I branch rosemary

6 tablespoons unsalted butter

1/3 cup extra-virgin olive oil

12 pieces Tomato Confit
   (see page 186), or use one 8-ounce
   can whole plum tomatoes, halved,
   drained, seeded, and thinly sliced

3 tablespoons minced flat-leaf
   or curly parsley

Juice of 1/2 lemon

** Alternate soaking method: If you don't
have time to soak the beans overnight, try
this quick-soak method: Place the beans
in a medium casserole and cover with warm
water 2 inches above the surface of the
beans. Bring to a boil over high heat, cover,
remove from the heat, and let stand for I to
I 1/2 hours. The beans will swell to twice
their volume. Drain.*

*France's southwest inspires this rustic, satisfying dish, with its grilled cod and savory,
herb-scented white beans with tomatoes. You can also serve the beans mashed or
processed into a purée. You'll need to start this dish up to three hours in advance to salt
the fish and cook the beans.*

Combine the coarse salt and the sugar in a small bowl, then spread half the mixture
on a large dinner plate. Place the fillets on top of the salt mixture, then cover them
with the remaining salt mixture. Cover the plate with plastic wrap and refrigerate
the fillets for I 1/2 hours.

Rinse the fillets well with cold water to remove all the salt mixture and dry well
with paper towels. Season both sides well with freshly ground pepper, and set
aside.

Meanwhile, combine the beans with 1/4 teaspoon of salt and enough water to cover
by 2 inches in a large pot. Bring to a boil over high heat, and add the rosemary and
sage. Reduce the heat to medium and cook until the beans are tender, I to I 1/2
hours. Set the pot aside and allow the beans to cool in their cooking liquid. Drain the
beans, reserving the cooking liquid. Transfer the beans (along with the sage leaves
and rosemary) to a large skillet with 1/3 cup of the cooking liquid, and warm over
medium heat. Add 3 tablespoons of butter, I tablespoon of olive oil, and salt and
pepper to taste and stir to combine. (If you would like to purée the beans, do it
at this point, mashing them well with a fork, or placing them in a food processor
and pulsing until smooth; if the mixture is too thick, add a few tablespoons of the
reserved cooking liquid and pulse.) Add the tomatoes and stir gently to combine.
Keep warm over low heat.

Melt the remaining 3 tablespoons of the butter over medium heat. Add the parsley,
lemon juice, and a pinch of salt and stir to combine. Cook for I minute, just until
the parsley begins to wilt. Remove from the heat and set aside.

Heat the remaining 1/4 cup of olive oil in a large cast-iron or other heavy-bottomed
skillet over medium heat. Add the cod fillets, season with salt and pepper, and cook
until golden brown, about 5 minutes on each side. Divide the fillets among four
warmed serving plates and drizzle with the parsley butter. Spoon the beans next
to the fillets and serve.

Sea Bass in Herb Butter with Chanterelles

Serves **6**

For the herb butter

12 tablespoons (1 1/2 sticks)
  salted butter, softened
1 teaspoon grated lemon zest
1/4 cup slivered almonds,
  finely chopped
1/4 cup finely chopped walnuts
10 garlic cloves, minced
1 tablespoon whole-grain mustard
1 slice (about 1 ounce) Serrano or
  prosciutto ham, minced
3 tablespoons minced fresh herbs
  (choose 2 or 3 among chervil,
  chives, and parsley)
Freshly ground black pepper

For the mushroom garnish

3 tablespoons extra-virgin olive oil
8 plum tomatoes, peeled, quartered,
  and seeded; or one 8-ounce can
  peeled Italian plum tomatoes,
  drained, quartered, and seeded
6 cloves Garlic Confit (see page 187)
8 ounces whole chanterelle
  mushrooms, or cremini
  mushrooms, trimmed
1/4 cup chopped fresh basil leaves
Fine sea salt
Freshly ground black pepper

For the sea bass

6 fillets of sea bass (approximately
  6 ounces each)
Fine sea salt
Freshly ground black pepper
Fleur de sel, or coarse sea salt
6 sprigs basil for garnish

Crushed walnuts and almonds add a touch of sweetness to the lovely green herb butter that blankets these sea bass fillets. Note that the recipe calls for Garlic Confit, which needs one and a half hours of slow baking before you proceed with this recipe.

To prepare the herb butter

Cream the butter in a large bowl, then add the remaining ingredients, season with pepper, and stir well to combine. Cover and refrigerate until ready to use.

To prepare the mushroom garnish

Heat 2 tablespoons of the olive oil in a large skillet over medium-high heat, add the tomatoes and garlic, stir to combine, then cook until all the liquid has evaporated, about 3 minutes. Transfer to a bowl and keep warm in a low oven. Add the remaining olive oil to the skillet, warm for 1 minute, add the mushrooms and cook, stirring frequently, for 3 minutes, until the mushrooms soften slightly. Add the chopped basil leaves, season with salt and pepper, and stir to combine. Keep warm over very low heat until ready to serve.

To prepare the sea bass and serve

Preheat the oven to 450°F. Sprinkle the fillets with salt and pepper and arrange them in a single layer on a baking pan with 1-inch sides. Spread the herb butter over the top of the fillets and bake them in the oven for 8 minutes, until the fillets are cooked through and flaky. Do not overcook. Divide the fillets among six warmed serving plates. Spoon the mushrooms on one side of the fillets, the tomato mixture on the other side. Sprinkle with coarse sea salt, garnish with the basil, and serve immediately.

[Colin au Chutney de Pignon]

Hake with Pine Nut Chutney

Serves **6**

Hake is a mild, delicately textured, white-fleshed fish from the western Atlantic that pairs very well with an assertive, flavorful accompaniment such as this Pine Nut Chutney. The chutney has a base of spinach and watercress studded with raisins, capers, pine nuts, and olives. A garnish of asparagus, baby onions, and boiled potatoes add flavor contrast and eye appeal. Note that the recipe calls for Garlic Confit, which needs one and a half hours of slow baking.

For the pine nut chutney

1/4 cup currants
2 tablespoons extra-virgin olive oil
1 bunch watercress, stems removed
 and discarded
1 head butterhead or Boston lettuce,
 cored, leaves separated
One 4-ounce package baby spinach
 leaves
1/4 cup pine nuts
1 1/2 tablespoon capers
1/2 cup pitted Niçoise olives,
 or other small, brined-cured
 black olives
Fine sea salt
Freshly ground black pepper

For the vegetable garnish

30 small red new potatoes,
 peeled and quartered
18 pearl onions, peeled
30 asparagus tips, fresh or frozen

For the hake

6 hake steaks (approximately
 6 ounces each), or use hake fillets
 with skin on
Fine sea salt
Freshly ground black pepper
1 cup all-purpose flour
3 tablespoons extra-virgin olive oil
6 cloves Garlic Confit (see page 187)
1 tablespoon capers
2 tablespoons balsamic vinegar
2 tablespoons unsalted butter

To prepare the chutney

Place the currants in a small bowl, cover with warm water, and set aside for about 5 minutes to plump a bit. Heat the olive oil in a large skillet over medium-high heat. Add the watercress, lettuce, spinach, and 2 tablespoons of water, and stir to combine. Cover and cook, stirring occasionally, until the leaves are wilted, approximately 3 minutes. Drain the leaves, pressing gently to remove the water. Chop the leaves coarsely with a knife, transfer to a large bowl, and set aside. Drain the currants and set aside.

Toast the pine nuts in a medium skillet over medium heat, stirring continuously, until lightly browned, about 3 minutes. Add the pine nuts, drained currants, capers, and olives to the wilted greens, and stir to combine. Season to taste with salt and pepper, and set aside.

To prepare the vegetable garnish

Bring a large stockpot of salted water to a boil over high heat. Add the potatoes and cook for 5 minutes. Add the onions and asparagus and cook for 5 minutes more. Drain and set aside.

To serve

Preheat the oven to 175°F. Season the hake fillets with salt and pepper, then flour them lightly on both sides, shaking off the excess. Heat the olive oil in a large skillet over medium-high heat, add the hake and cook for 2 minutes on each side. Add the vegetable garnish and cover. Cook for about 10 minutes, shaking the pan occasionally, until the hake flakes easily with a fork. With a metal spatula, carefully transfer the hake and vegetable garnish to a warmed platter, cover with foil, and keep warm in the oven. Reduce the heat to medium, add the garlic cloves, capers, and vinegar to the skillet, stir to combine, and cook over medium heat for 2 minutes. Add the butter a little at a time, stirring until incorporated. Season to taste with salt and pepper. Remove from the heat, set aside, and keep warm.

Reheat the chutney over medium heat, stirring occasionally, until heated through, about 2 minutes. Divide the chutney among six warmed serving plates. Place a hake steak atop each serving, and arrange the vegetables around the border of the plate, reserving a few asparagus tips and capers to garnish the top of the fish. Drizzle with the vinegar mixture and serve.

Fish

Serves **6**

For the Biscayenne sauce

6 slices cured Serrano or prosciutto
  ham
3 tablespoon extra-virgin olive oil
I medium onion, thinly sliced
One 6-ounce can of Pimientos
  del Piquillo, or other pimientos,
  drained and cut into thin strips
5 garlic cloves, crushed
I branch thyme
I bay leaf
5 branches basil leaves,
  finely julienned, stems reserved
One 15-ounce can chopped
  tomatoes
Fine sea salt
Freshly ground black pepper
Pinch of ground saffron

For the tuna

6 fresh tuna steaks
  (approximately 5 ounces each)
1/2 cup extra-virgin olive oil
3 garlic cloves, peeled and chopped
I branch rosemary
I branch thyme
I bay leaf
1/2 teaspoon ground Piment
  d'Espelette (a Basque chili pepper)
  or 1/2 teaspoon ground cayenne
  pepper
Fleur de sel, or coarse sea salt
Freshly ground black pepper

For the garnish

3 thin slices of cured Serrano
  or prosciutto ham
6 sliced fresh basil leaves
18 pieces Tomato Confit
  (see page 186), or sun-dried
  tomatoes in oil, drained
3 tablespoons extra-virgin olive oil
Fleur de sel, or coarse sea salt
Freshly ground black pepper

This is a dish inspired by the fish-based cooking in the Bay of Biscay, a lively area in France's southwestern Basque country. The recipe's name derives from the Bay. Tuna Biscayenne, with a zesty sauce that enlivens the rich, succulent fish, is served at room temperature, and so can be prepared well ahead of serving. The sauce cooks for an hour and a half, and the tuna marinates for an hour, so you'll need to start this dish in mid-afternoon for dinnertime.

To prepare the Biscayenne sauce

Preheat the oven to 275°F. Trim the fat from the ham and reserve. Slice the ham into thin strips. In a medium casserole over medium-high heat, heat the olive oil. Add the onion and sauté for 2 minutes, stirring frequently. Reduce the heat to low, cover, and cook about 15 minutes, stirring occasionally, until the onions are soft and translucent. Add the pimientos, reserved ham fat, garlic, thyme, bay leaf, and the basil stems and stir to combine. Cook for 2 minutes.

Add the chopped tomatoes, a pinch of salt, and freshly ground pepper and stir to combine. Cover and cook in the center of the oven for 1 1/2 hours. Remove from the oven and place over low heat on the stovetop. Remove and discard the basil stems, thyme, and bay leaf. Add the ham strips, julienned basil, and saffron and stir to combine. Cover and cook on low heat for 10 minutes. Season to taste, then transfer the mixture to a shallow baking dish and set aside to cool.

To prepare the tuna

Coat the tuna steaks with olive oil and place in a large mixing bowl. Add the garlic, rosemary, thyme, bay leaf, and Piment d'Espelette. Season with a pinch of salt and freshly ground pepper. Cover the dish with plastic wrap and set aside in the refrigerator to marinate for 1 hour.

Remove the herbs, transfer the tuna to a platter, and wipe any excess oil from the steaks with paper towels. In a large skillet over high heat, sear the steaks for 2 minutes on each side. Place the tuna steaks on top of the Biscayenne sauce and let cool.

To prepare the garnish and serve

In the bowl of a food processor, combine the ham, basil, tomatoes, and oil. Pulse until finely chopped. Divide the Biscayenne sauce among six deep serving plates or shallow soup bowls. Top each serving with a tuna steak, garnish with the ham mixture, sprinkle with fleur de sel and freshly ground black pepper, and serve.

[Darioles de Crevettes]

Shrimp Darioles

Serves **6**

For the shrimp darioles

1/2 pound fresh or frozen shrimp,
  peeled, shells reserved
3 large egg yolks
I whole large egg
I cup heavy cream
1/2 cup whole milk
1/4 teaspoon ground nutmeg
Fine sea salt
Freshly ground black pepper

For the sauce

3 tablespoons unsalted butter
Shrimp shells
2 garlic cloves, peeled and crushed
2 tablespoons cognac
2 cups fish stock (or substitute
  I 1/2 cups chicken stock mixed
  with 1/2 cup clam juice)
1/2 bunch basil, stems removed
4 tablespoons salted butter, cubed
Fine sea salt
Freshly ground black pepper
12 medium shrimp, boiled and
  peeled, optional for garnish

These airy shrimp custards, similar to a mousse, are named for a classic French cylindrical mold often used for creating pastries. The dish would be a perfect starter for an elegant dinner. The darioles cook best in a large 6-cup silicone muffin mold.

To prepare the darioles

Preheat the oven to 325°F. Place the shrimp in the bowl of a food processor and purée until the mixture forms a paste. Add the egg yolks, egg, cream, milk, nutmeg, and a generous pinch of salt and pepper and purée until blended. Pour the mixture into the cups of a 6-cup silicone muffin mold, or use a 6-cup nonstick muffin pan. Place the mold, or the muffin pan, into a baking dish large enough to hold it, then fill halfway with water. Bake the *darioles* in the center of the oven for 50 minutes, just until the middle of each is set. Transfer the mold to a wire rack to cool.

To prepare the sauce

In a medium saucepan, melt the unsalted butter over medium-high heat. Add the shrimp shells and garlic, and cook, stirring occasionally, for 5 minutes. Add the cognac and stir to combine. Add the fish stock and basil, stir, then reduce the heat to low and simmer, stirring occasionally, for 20 minutes. Strain the sauce through a fine-mesh strainer, or a colander lined with 3 layers of cheesecloth, into a medium saucepan. Reduce the mixture over high heat, stirring frequently, until it begins to thicken, about 7 minutes. Whisk in the butter, a little at a time, until combined. Taste and adjust the seasoning if necessary.

To serve

Reheat the *darioles* for I minute in the microwave. Place each on a warmed serving plate and drizzle the sauce around. Garnish each serving with basil leaves, or, if you wish, 2 boiled shrimp.

Fish

[Tarte Fine aux Anchois]

Anchovy Tart

Serves **6**

One 17-ounce package (2 sheets)
  commercial puff pastry dough
3 tomatoes, peeled, seeded,
  and cut into 6 wedges
1/2 teaspoon fine sea salt
30 fillets of fresh anchovies,
  meticulously boned, marinated
  overnight in the refrigerator
  in extra-virgin olive oil to cover
Freshly ground black pepper
1/2 cup Provençal Olive Paste
  (see page 189)
1 tablespoon extra-virgin olive oil
3 to 4 sprigs basil, leaves picked,
  stems removed, optional
  for garnish

This vibrant, assertively flavored tart is a composition of classic Mediterranean ingredients. You need to begin preparations a day ahead, since the fresh anchovy fillets (have your fish monger prepare them) must be marinated in olive oil for about twenty-four hours. The released tomato water can be used—as it is by some of Mr. Ducasse's chefs—to make a tasty Tomato Vinaigrette (see page 189).

Preheat the oven to 350°F. On a floured work surface, roll one sheet of the dough out to a 12 by 10-inch rectangle. Repeat with the other sheet. Using an inverted 5- to 6-inch bowl as a guide, cut out 3 pastry circles from each sheet. Line a baking sheet with parchment paper and arrange the pastry circles on top. Cover them with another sheet of parchment paper, then with a second baking sheet the same size as the first or just slightly smaller. This second baking sheet serves as a weight to keep the pastry from rising too much. Bake the pastry circles for 20 minutes. Transfer the circles to a wire rack to cool for 15 to 20 minutes. Raise the oven temperature to 375°F.

Place the tomato wedges in a strainer and sprinkle the salt; this helps the tomatoes release some of their water. Set aside over a bowl to drain for approximately 10 minutes. Drain the anchovies and dry thoroughly. Pat the tomato slices with paper towels to absorb any excess moisture. Return the pastry circles to a baking sheet covered with parchment paper. Arrange the 6 tomato wedges on each pastry disk in a star pattern. Top each serving with 5 anchovy fillets in the same pattern. Sprinkle with pepper and spread with the tapenade. Drizzle lightly with olive oil, then bake in the oven for 5 minutes, or until the crust browns slightly and the topping is just heated through.

Decorate with basil leaves, if you wish, and serve immediately.

Meats and Poultry

Spiced Rack of Lamb with Onion Sauce

Roasted Lamb Shanks with Citrus Crust

Filet of Beef Bordelaise

Rib-eye Steak with Shallot Sauce and French Fries

Veal Saltimbocca

Roast Rack of Pork with Sautéed Apples and Sausages

Veal Medallions with Tomato Sauce

Caramelized Veal Shank

Calf's Liver Florentine

Fricassee of Veal Kidneys in Dijon Mustard Sauce

Rolled Stuffed Escalope of Turkey with Musxtard Sauce

Grilled Duck Breasts with Red Wine and Orange Sauce

Sautéed Fresh Foie Gras with Apples and Grapes

Chicken Breasts Pojarski

Chicken Fricassee

Garlic-Roasted Cornish Hens with Cherry Sauce

For the onion sauce

5 medium red onions, finely minced

3 tablespoons extra-virgin olive oil

3/4 teaspoon finely ground white
   pepper

3/4 teaspoon ground cinnamon

3/4 teaspoon ground nutmeg

3/4 teaspoon ground cloves

2 garlic cloves, peeled and crushed

Zest of 2 lemons

Fleur de sel, or coarse sea salt

Freshly ground black pepper

1/4 cup veal or chicken stock

For the garnish

2 tablespoons unsalted butter

24 whole almonds, lightly crushed

6 dried apricots, halved

2 garlic cloves, peeled and halved

1/2 cup golden raisins

2 branches thyme

1 cup veal or chicken stock

2 tablespoons capers

1 jar of Pimientos del Piquillo
   peppers, or 1 whole canned
   pimiento, strained and cut into
   bits

Fine sea salt

Freshly ground black pepper

For the racks of lamb

Two 7- or 8-rib racks of lamb
   (about 2 pounds each)

Fleur de sel, or coarse sea salt

4 branches thyme, leaves picked

2 garlic cloves, peeled

Freshly ground black pepper

2 tablespoons extra-virgin olive oil

1/4 cup chopped flat-leaf parsley
   or cilantro

[Carré d'Agneau aux Épices]

Spiced Rack of Lamb with Onion Sauce

Serves **6**

In this delicious rack of lamb recipe, the dried fruit and almond garnish, as well as the spicy caramelized red-onion sauce, add great contrasting flavor and texture to the rich, roasted meat.

To prepare the onion sauce

Preheat the oven to 250°F. In a large, ovenproof skillet, heat the oil over high heat, then add the onions and stir to combine. Reduce the heat to medium and cook, stirring occasionally, until the onions are translucent but not browned, about 3 minutes. In a small bowl, combine the white pepper, cinnamon, nutmeg, and cloves. Add the mixture to the onions, along with the garlic, lemon zest, and a pinch of salt and pepper. and stir to combine. Cover, place in the center of the oven, and cook for 1 hour, stirring occasionally. Carefully remove from the oven and place the skillet on the top of the stove over medium heat. Continue to cook the onions, stirring frequently, until lightly browned, 5 to 7 minutes. Add the veal stock, season to taste, and stir to combine. Transfer the mixture to a food processor and process until smooth. Set aside.

To prepare the garnish

In a medium skillet, melt the butter over medium heat. Add the almonds, apricots, garlic, raisins, and thyme and stir to combine. Cook for 1 minute, stirring occasionally. Add the veal stock, stir to combine, reduce the heat to low, and simmer, stirring occasionally, for 15 minutes. Remove from the heat, stir in the capers and the pimientos. Season to taste and set aside.

To prepare the racks of lamb

Preheat the oven to 475°F. Rub each rack of lamb with fleur de sel, thyme, and garlic. Sprinkle with pepper, and place the racks in a roasting pan. Drizzle the racks with olive oil and place in the center of the oven. Roast for 10 minutes, reduce the heat to 400°F and roast about 15 minutes more for medium-rare. Remove the racks from the oven, cover with a sheet of aluminum foil, and let rest for at least 5 minutes before cutting.

To serve

Slice the racks into individual chops. Divide the fruit garnish among six warmed serving plates, mounding each portion in the center, and place 2 or 3 chops on top of the garnish. Drizzle the caramelized onion sauce around the racks, and sprinkle with fleur de sel and a bit of chopped parsley or cilantro. Serve immediately.

[Souris d'Agneau aux Agrumes]

Roasted Lamb Shanks with Citrus Crust

Serves **6**

For the citrus crust

1 orange, zested and juiced
1 lemon, zested and juiced
1/2 grapefruit, zested and juiced
2 tablespoons sugar
10 tablespoons (1 1/4 sticks)
    unsalted butter, softened
1/2 cup plain dried bread crumbs
1 tablespoon whole-grain mustard
1 tablespoon extra-virgin olive oil
Fine sea salt
Freshly ground black pepper

For the lamb shanks

2 tablespoons extra-virgin olive oil
3 lamb shanks (about 1 pound each)
Fine sea salt
Freshly ground black pepper
Zest of 1 orange for garnish

Here is a contemporary take on a French farmhouse classic—breaded lamb shanks. In this recipe, the crust is spiked with zested orange, lemon, and grapefruit, a combination that adds a nice contrast to the richness of the meat. The crust also makes a delicious coating for a leg of lamb. Serve with the Mille-feuilles of Crispy Potatoes (page 128), or a potato purée.

To prepare the citrus crust

Finely mince the citrus zests, place them in a small strainer, then dip them into a pot of boiling water and blanch for 30 seconds. Drain and pat dry. Combine the zests with the citrus juices and sugar in a medium saucepan, bring to a boil over medium-high heat, and cook, stirring occasionally. Reduce the mixture over high heat, stirring frequently, until it thickens, about 7 minutes. Combine the citrus mixture with the butter, bread crumbs, mustard, and olive oil in a medium bowl, and stir until the mixture forms a smooth paste. Season to taste with salt and pepper and set aside.

To prepare the lamb shanks

Preheat the oven to 450°F. Heat the olive oil in a large skillet over medium-high heat. Season the lamb shanks with salt and pepper, then sear until golden brown on all sides. Liberally coat the shanks with the reserved citrus crust mixture, then carefully transfer them to a greased baking pan. Press any remaining crust mixture onto the shanks, then place them in the center of the oven and bake for 5 minutes. Reduce the heat to 400°F and bake 30 minutes, basting frequently with the drippings.

Place a lamb shank on each of six warmed serving plates, drizzle with a bit of the pan drippings, garnish with strips of orange zest, if you wish, and serve.

[Filet de Bœuf et sa Sauce Bordelaise]

Filet of Beef Bordelaise

Serves **6**

2 marrowbones

1 tablespoon white vinegar

3 shallots, peeled and chopped

1 tablespoon sugar

1 branch thyme

1 bay leaf

1 bottle dry red wine

2 cups veal or chicken stock

3 sticks plus 2 tablespoons unsalted
  butter, cut into bits

1/3 cup heavy cream

Fine sea salt

Freshly ground black pepper

Six 1-inch-thick filet mignons
  (about 6 ounces each)

2 tablespoons sunflower oil

Fleur de sel, or coarse sea salt

Filet mignon and a cream-based, red-wine sauce make for a perfect marriage. Marrow from beef marrowbones makes the sauce even more savory. Watch the wine carefully as it reduces, since it can easily burn with just a few too many seconds of heat. Serve with a Potato and Ham Gratin (page 134), or with steamed haricots verts tossed with Garlic-Shallot Butter (page 187).

Submerge the marrowbones in a bowl of very cold water combined with the vinegar, and set aside for 15 minutes; this will eliminate impurities in the marrow. Bring a medium pot of water to a rolling boil over high heat. Add the marrowbones and boil for 30 seconds. Strain and gently remove the marrow from the bones. Thinly slice the marrow and set aside. Discard the bones.

Combine the shallots, sugar, thyme, and bay leaf in a large saucepan. Add the bottle of red wine and bring to a boil over high heat. Lower the heat to medium-high, and reduce the mixture until approximately 1/2 cup remains. Add the veal stock and stir to blend. Strain the mixture through a fine-mesh strainer, then return it to the saucepan. Reduce the mixture over high heat, stirring frequently, until it becomes slightly thickened, about 5 minutes. Whisk in the 3 sticks of butter a few pieces at a time, then incorporate the marrow and cream, whisking to blend. Adjust the seasoning to taste. Keep warm over low heat until ready to use.

With paper towels (ideally unbleached), dry the surfaces of the meat. (The drier the meat is, the better it will sear.) In a large skillet, combine the remaining 2 tablespoons of butter with the sunflower oil and heat over high heat, stirring to blend, until the butter melts. Sprinkle the filets with salt and pepper. When the pan is hot, sear the filets according to your preference, about 4 minutes per side for medium-rare. Place the filets on warmed serving plates, sprinkle with fleur de sel, and drizzle the sauce over and around the meat. Serve immediately.

[Entrecôte-frites]

Rib-eye Steak with Shallot Sauce and French Fries

Serves **4**

For the shallot-red wine sauce

12 shallots, minced
3 garlic cloves, peeled, crushed
1 branch thyme
1/2 cup olive oil
2 cups dry red wine
2 tablespoons unsalted butter,
  chilled, cut into bits
Fine sea salt
Freshly ground black pepper

For the French fries

4 large russet potatoes, skin on,
  cut lengthwise into 1/3-inch slices,
  then cut each slice
  into 1/3-inch-wide strips
Canola oil, or other vegetable oil,
  for deep-frying
Fine sea salt
Freshly ground black pepper

For the rib-eye steak

4 tablespoons canola or sunflower
  oil
3 tablespoons unsalted butter
2 boneless rib-eye steaks
  (about 16 ounces each)
Fine sea salt
Freshly ground black pepper
Coarse sea salt

Steak-frites is a beloved French bistro classic. Here we use a rib-eye steak, a well-marbled cut, bathed in a shallot-red wine reduction sauce. The "frites"—French fries—are crunchy on the outside, tender on the inside, twice-fried as the best fries always are. The two pounds of meat called for is intended to serve four.

To prepare the shallot fondue

Preheat the oven to 250°F. Heat the olive oil in a large ovenproof skillet over medium-high heat. Add the garlic cloves, thyme, and shallots, and stir to combine. Cover the skillet and bake in the center of the oven for 1 hour, stirring once or twice, until the shallots are soft. Remove the shallots from the oven, drain the excess fat from the skillet, then place the skillet with the shallots over medium-high heat. Add the wine and stir to combine. Reduce the heat to medium, and cook until the mixture thickens and reduces to about 3/4 cup, 7 to 10 minutes. Whisk in the butter bit by bit and season to taste with salt and pepper. Keep warm over very low heat.

To prepare the French fries

Place the potatoes in a large bowl filled with cold water and let sit for 20 minutes to remove the starch. Drain and dry well. Fill a deep fryer or other large, deep, heavy-bottomed pot with sides at least 8 inches high with 3 inches of canola oil. Heat to 325°F. Add the potatoes 1 cup at a time and cook for about 5 minutes, until they stop spattering and are lightly browned. Using a slotted spoon, transfer the half-cooked fries to paper towels to drain. Reserve the fries at this point and proceed to cook the steak before the second frying.

To prepare the rib-eye steaks

Season the steaks on both sides with salt and pepper, and set aside. Combine the butter and oil in a large skillet over high heat and stir to blend. When the butter is melted and bubbling, add the steaks, reduce the heat to medium, and cook, basting occasionally with the butter mixture, 5 to 6 minutes on each side for medium-rare. Transfer to a carving board and let rest for 5 minutes before serving.

To finish and serve

Meanwhile, complete the second frying of the potatoes. While the steak is resting and just before serving, heat the oil to 365°F. Add the potatoes and fry in batches until crisp and golden, 2 to 3 minutes. With a slotted spoon or fry basket, lift the fries out and drain on paper towels. Sprinkle with salt and serve immediately. Slice the steak across the grain (like London broil) and divide among four warmed serving dishes. Top the slices with the reserved shallot-red wine sauce, sprinkle with coarse sea salt, and serve with the French fries.

[Veau à la Saltimbocca]

Veal Saltimbocca

Serves **6**

For the garnish

8 tablespoons (1 stick) unsalted
   butter
30 pearl onions, boiled for 1 minute,
   then peeled
1/2 teaspoon fine sea salt
1/8 teaspoon freshly ground black
   pepper
1 teaspoon sugar
2 pinches dried oregano
12 sun-dried tomatoes in oil, drained
One 15-ounce can of tomato purée
1/4 cup veal or chicken stock
Fine sea salt
Freshly ground black pepper

For the bread-crumb mixture

2 large eggs
1/2 cup milk
3 tablespoons extra-virgin olive oil
Freshly ground black pepper
1 cup all-purpose flour
1 cup bread crumbs
Fine sea salt

For the veal

2 pounds veal scaloppini slices
   (about 16 to 20), cut 1/4 inch thick,
   then pounded slightly thinner
Fine sea salt
Freshly ground black pepper
4 tablespoons unsalted butter
1 carrot, peeled and diced small
1 onion, peeled and diced small
1 celery stalk, diced small
1/2 cup veal or chicken stock
9 large, thin slices (about 1/4 pound)
   cured Serrano or prosciutto ham
9 fresh sage leaves, halved
2 tablespoons extra-virgin olive oil

In this delicious French interpretation of the classic Italian veal dish, in which the veal usually encloses the ham, sage, and vegetable filling, it is the ham that wraps the veal and other components. Breading on one side of each saltimbocca roll adds a lovely, crunchy texture.

To prepare the garnish

In a medium skillet, melt the butter over medium-high heat. Add the onions, salt, pepper, and sugar and cook for 10 minutes, stirring occasionally. Add the oregano and the sun-dried tomatoes and stir to combine. Remove from the heat and set aside. In a medium saucepan, combine the tomato purée and veal stock, and heat to a simmer over medium-high heat. Taste and adjust the seasoning, remove from the heat, and set aside.

To prepare the bread-crumb mixture

In a large mixing bowl, combine the eggs, milk, and oil. Add a pinch of salt and pepper and beat to blend. Place the flour on one large plate and the bread crumbs on another. Set the bowl and two plates aside.

To prepare the veal

Sprinkle the veal with salt and freshly ground pepper and set aside. In a large skillet, melt 2 tablespoons of the butter over medium heat, then add the carrots, onion, and celery and stir to combine. Cook for 3 minutes, stirring frequently, until the vegetables soften and onions begin to look translucent but not brown. Add the veal stock to the mixture and stir to combine. Reduce the heat to low and cook, stirring occasionally, for 10 minutes. Remove the skillet from the heat and set aside.

Spread the ham slices on a flat surface and cut each in half, making 18 pieces. Onto each ham slice, place about 1 tablespoon of the vegetable mixture, a sage leaf half, and a piece of veal scaloppini. Roll the ham snugly around the filling, secure with a toothpick, and set aside.

Preheat the oven to 200°F. Work in batches to cook the veal saltimbocca rolls; keep finished portions warm in the oven until ready to serve. Dip one side of each saltimbocca roll in the flour, then in the egg mixture, and finally in the bread crumbs. In a large skillet, heat the remaining 2 tablespoons of butter and 2 tablespoons of oil over medium-high heat. When the butter is melted and bubbling, place the saltimbocca roll breaded side down in the pan. Cook for about 3 minutes, or until golden brown. Turn the rolls over, lower the heat to medium-low, cover, and cook about 10 minutes, or until the bottom of each roll is golden brown and the filling is cooked through.

Meanwhile, reheat the onion garnish and the tomato sauce over medium heat. Divide the onion garnish among six heated plates. Place 3 saltimbocca rolls atop each serving and drizzle with the tomato sauce. Serve immediately.

[Carré de Porc Rôti aux Boudins Noirs]

Roast Rack of Pork with Sautéed Apples and Sausages

Serves **6**

For the rack of pork

One 8-bone rack of pork
  (about 5 pounds), chine bone
  removed
1/2 cup extra-virgin olive oil
2 tablespoons chopped fresh thyme
Fine sea salt
Freshly ground black pepper
Fleur de sel, or coarse sea salt

For the sautéed apples
and sausage

4 tablespoons unsalted butter
3 Golden Delicious apples, peeled,
  cored, and quartered
2 tablespoons Calvados,
  or other apple brandy
4 tablespoons extra-virgin olive oil
1/4 pound slab bacon, diced
2 medium white onions,
  minced
Freshly ground black pepper
2 blood sausages, sliced
  (or substitute andouille or mild
  Italian sausage)
Fine sea salt

Here's a hearty meal for a winter's night—roast pork with savory sautéed apples and sausage. While the recipe calls for the French specialty boudin noir—blood sausages—produced here by Schaller and Weber and some other local butchers, you can also use andouille sausages or mild Italian sausage. Serve, if you wish, with an Eggplant Purée (page 190), an accompaniment that makes a nice counterpoint to the richness of the pork and apples.

To prepare the rack of pork

Preheat the oven to 350°F. Stand the rack in a roasting pan, rib-bone side up, and coat thoroughly with the olive oil. Sprinkle with the thyme and season generously with fine sea salt and pepper. Position the oven rack in the bottom third of the oven. Roast the pork for 1 1/2 hours, or until the internal temperature reaches 160°F for medium, about 10 degrees less if you prefer the pork slightly pink. Remove the pan from the oven, cover the roast with foil, and set aside to rest for 15 to 20 minutes. Reserve the pan drippings.

Meanwhile, prepare the apples and sausage

Melt the butter in a large skillet, over medium-high heat. Add the apples, reduce the heat to medium, and sauté, stirring frequently, until browned on all sides, about 7 minutes. Add the Calvados, stir to combine, cook 1 minute more, then set aside.

Heat 2 tablespoons of the olive oil in a medium skillet over medium heat, add the bacon and onions, and stir to combine. Sauté, stirring occasionally, until the onions are soft and translucent, about 10 minutes. Season with pepper, then add the mixture to the reserved apples.

Warm the remaining 2 tablespoons of olive oil in a medium skillet over medium heat, add the sausage slices and sauté, stirring occasionally, until cooked through. Add to the apple mixture, toss gently to combine, and set aside.

To serve

Slice the roast between the ribs into chops and divide among six warmed serving plates, then spoon some of the apple and sausage mixture next to the pork. Serve with eggplant purée, if you wish, in a separate small bowl, or place a helping on the plate with the pork and apple mixture. Drizzle with a bit of the pan drippings, sprinkle with a pinch of fleur de sel, and serve immediately.

[Médaillons de Veau en Grenadin]

Veal Medallions with Tomato Sauce

Serves **6**

For the sauce

One 15-ounce can tomato purée
2 garlic cloves, crushed
1 tablespoon tomato paste
1 teaspoon sugar
1 cup veal or chicken stock
10 fresh basil leaves, coarsely
   chopped
Fine sea salt
Freshly ground black pepper

For the veal medallions

2 tablespoons extra-virgin olive oil
6 veal medallions
   (about 6 ounces each)
Fine sea salt
Freshly ground black pepper
5 tablespoons unsalted butter
2 garlic cloves, crushed
1 sprig thyme
12 whole almonds, coarsely chopped

Ready in just forty minutes, this tender veal dish with a garlicky tomato sauce is very easy to prepare, and very tasty!

To prepare the sauce

Combine the tomato purée and garlic in a large skillet over medium-high heat and stir to combine. Simmer, stirring frequently, until all of the liquid evaporates, about 7 minutes. Add the tomato paste and sugar, and mix to incorporate. Add the stock and cook until the sauce thickens and reduces to 1/2 cup, about 10 minutes. Add the basil and season with salt and pepper. Keep warm over low heat until ready to use.

To prepare the veal medallions

Heat the oil in a large skillet over medium heat. Season both sides of the veal with salt and pepper, place in the skillet, and sauté until browned, about 2 minutes on each side. Add the butter, garlic, and thyme, and cook, basting the veal with the cooking juices, 4 more minutes for medium-rare.

Place a medallion on each of six serving plates, spoon the sauce around the medallions, sprinkle with the almonds, and serve.

[Jarret de Veau Caramelisé]

Caramelized Veal Shank

Serves **6**

3 tablespoons extra-virgin olive oil
2 veal shanks
3 carrots, peeled and sliced
2 medium white onions,
  peeled and sliced
2 garlic cloves, peeled and crushed
1/2 cup red wine vinegar
4 tablespoons honey
2 cups veal or chicken stock
2 sprigs thyme
Fine sea salt
Freshly ground black pepper

This rustic, mouthwatering veal dish takes only ten minutes to prepare before it cooks slowly in the oven, absorbing the flavors of honey, vinegar, and herbs, for two hours. You finish the cooking on the stovetop. Serve with a potato purée, or fork-mashed potatoes drizzled with olive oil and sprinkled with fleur de sel, or coarse sea salt.

Preheat the oven to 325ºF. In a large ovenproof skillet with a lid, heat the olive oil over high heat. Add the shanks and brown on all sides, about 3 minutes per side. Remove the shanks and add the carrots, onions, and garlic and stir to combine. Sauté for 5 minutes, until the vegetables begin to brown, stirring frequently. Add the vinegar and stir to coat the vegetables. Return the shanks to the skillet and add the honey, stock, and thyme. Season with salt and pepper and stir well. Cover and bake in the center of the oven for 2 hours.

Transfer the shanks from the skillet to a warmed platter and cover with aluminum foil. Strain the remaining liquid through a fine-mesh strainer into a small skillet and reduce over medium-high heat until the sauce thickens, about 10 minutes. Season to taste with salt and pepper. Place the reserved shanks back in the sauce, spooning the sauce over the meat to bathe it. Slice the shanks and divide among six warmed serving plates. Serve with mashed or puréed potatoes.

[Foie de Veau à la Florentine]

Calf's Liver Florentine

Serves **6**

For the sauce

2 tablespoons unsalted butter
2 shallots, finely chopped
Freshly ground black pepper
1 tablespoon honey
Juice of 1/2 lemon
1/4 cup dry white vermouth
   (preferably Noilly Prat)
1/4 cup balsamic vinegar
1/2 cup veal stock, or chicken stock
20 seedless green grapes
1 tablespoon capers
Zest of 1/2 lemon
Fleur de sel, or coarse sea salt

For the garnish

4 tablespoons unsalted butter
2 pounds spinach, washed
   and drained
1 garlic clove, peeled
4 cloves Garlic Confit (see page 187),
   coarsely chopped, optional
   for garnish
Fine sea salt
Freshly ground black pepper

For the liver

2 tablespoons duck fat, chicken fat,
   or unsalted butter
One 2-pound piece calf's liver,
   membrane removed
2 unpeeled garlic cloves, crushed
1 sprig thyme
1 bay leaf
1 sprig rosemary
Fleur de sel, or coarse sea salt
Freshly ground black pepper

For lovers of calf's liver, this is an extremely appealing dish. The liver, sautéed with garlic and herbs, crowns a mound of mouthwatering, sweet-and-sour spinach prepared with honey, balsamic vinegar, and vermouth. Have your butcher custom cut a 2-pound piece of liver for you. Otherwise, you can certainly use two 1-pound pieces. You can accompany this dish with a side of sautéed new potatoes.

To prepare the sauce

In a large saucepan over medium heat, melt the butter. Add the shallots and sauté with a dash of freshly ground pepper for about 2 minutes. Add the honey and stir to combine, cooking until the mixture caramelizes lightly, about 5 minutes. Add the lemon juice and the vermouth, stir to combine, and cook over high heat until the mixture reduces by half, about 3 minutes. Add the vinegar, stir to combine and again reduce by half. Add the veal stock and cook over low heat until the mixture reduces to a thick sauce, about 10 minutes. Remove from the heat, add the grapes, capers, and lemon zest, and stir to combine. Taste and adjust the seasoning. Set aside in the pan.

To prepare the garnish

Melt half of the butter over medium heat in a large sauté pan and cook until it turns a nutty brown color, about 2 minutes. Add half of the spinach. Stick the garlic clove on the end of a fork and stir the spinach as it wilts. After it wilts completely, season with a pinch of salt and pepper, then transfer to a colander to drain. Repeat the same process with the remaining half of the spinach. Discard the garlic, or save for another use, such as flavoring a vinaigrette. Transfer the spinach to a bowl and keep warm in a low oven.

To prepare the calf's liver

In a large, cast-iron pan, melt the duck fat over high heat. Place the liver in the center of the pan and surround with the garlic cloves, thyme, bay leaf, and rosemary. Brown on both sides, 7 to 8 minutes per side. Toss the garlic and herbs in the fat from time to time so they do not burn.

Meanwhile, reheat the reserved sauce over medium heat. Slice the calf's liver into 6 equal portions. Divide the spinach among six serving plates. If you are using the confit garlic cloves, scatter them over the spinach. Place the liver pieces over each mound of spinach and sprinkle with fleur de sel and pepper. Drizzle with some of the sauce and serve immediately.

[Rognons de Veau de Lait
en Fricassée à la Moutarde]

Fricassee of Veal Kidneys in Dijon Mustard Sauce

Serves **6**

For the mustard sauce

2 tablespoons extra-virgin olive oil

2 shallots, finely chopped

I cup dry white wine

I tablespoon coriander seeds

2 unpeeled garlic cloves

2 tablespoons chopped fresh
tarragon

3/4 cup veal or chicken stock

I teaspoon Dijon mustard

Fine sea salt

Freshly ground black pepper

For the veal kidneys

3 veal kidneys (approximately
I pound each), membrane and
fatty centers removed

Fine sea salt

Freshly ground black pepper

6 tablespoons unsalted butter

3 unpeeled garlic cloves

I teaspoon whole-grain mustard

1/2 cup heavy cream

2 tablespoons chopped fresh
tarragon

This is an elegant interpretation of a beloved French bistro classic. Coriander seeds, garlic, and tarragon give great depth of flavor to the Dijon mustard sauce. Serve with Macaroni Gratin (page 190), steamed rice, or boiled new potatoes.

To prepare the mustard sauce

Warm the olive oil in a medium skillet over low heat. Add the shallots and sauté, stirring frequently, until light golden brown, about 7 minutes. Add the white wine, coriander, garlic, and tarragon, and stir to combine. Raise the heat to medium and cook, stirring occasionally, until all the liquid has evaporated, about 8 minutes. Add the stock and cook, stirring occasionally, until the mixture reduces by half, about 5 minutes. Stir in the Dijon mustard, then strain the sauce into a bowl through a fine-mesh strainer. Return the sauce to the skillet, season with salt and pepper, and set aside.

To prepare the veal kidneys

Cut the kidneys crosswise into 3/4-inch slices, season with salt and pepper, and set aside. Melt the butter in a large skillet over medium-high heat, add the kidneys and garlic, and sauté for 3 minutes, stirring occasionally. Using a slotted spoon, transfer the kidney slices to the reserved mustard sauce, and stir to combine. Bring the mixture to a boil over medium-high heat and cook for 2 minutes, stirring frequently. Add the whole-grain mustard and cream, cook for another 2 minutes, stirring frequently. Adjust the seasoning if necessary. Divide the kidney fricassee among six warmed plates, sprinkle with chopped tarragon and serve.

[Roulade d'Escalope de Dinde Farcie]

Rolled Stuffed Escalope of Turkey with Mustard Sauce

Serves **6**

Here's a different and delicious way to prepare turkey—rolled in bacon, and stuffed with herbs, black olives, rosemary, and bacon bits. The mustard sauce, graced with tarragon and white wine, is just the right partner for this flavorful and satisfying dish. Serve with Macaroni Gratin (page 190).

For the stuffing

5 slices bacon, cooked until browned
  and crisp, coarsely chopped

5 sage leaves, coarsely chopped

1 tablespoon chopped fresh
  rosemary leaves

20 oil- or brine-cured imported black
  olives, pitted and chopped

For the turkey

18 thin slices bacon

6 turkey breast fillets (approximately
  1/2 pound each), pounded flat

Fine sea salt

Freshly ground black pepper

2 tablespoons unsalted butter

2 tablespoons extra-virgin olive oil

For the mustard sauce

2 shallots, peeled and minced

1 tablespoon chopped fresh tarragon

1/2 cup dry white wine

3 tablespoons unsalted butter,
  softened

2 teaspoons Dijon mustard

2 teaspoons whole-grain mustard

Freshly ground black pepper

To prepare the stuffing

Combine the bacon, sage, rosemary, and olives in a bowl, and set aside.

To prepare the turkey

On a cutting board, or other clean, flat work surface, lay out 3 slices of bacon side by side and slightly overlapping. Place 1 turkey fillet in the center of the bacon and season with salt and pepper. Place 2 to 3 tablespoons of the stuffing at one end of the fillet and roll the 3 layers closed, wrapping the turkey and stuffing inside the bacon slices. Secure by overlapping the ends of the bacon slices on the outside of the roll, fixing with a toothpick, then tying the roll with kitchen twine. Repeat with the remaining 5 turkey breasts.

Preheat the oven to 350°F. Melt the butter and olive oil in a large skillet over medium-high heat. Add the turkey rolls and sear until browned on all sides, 3 to 5 minutes. Cover the skillet, place in the center of the oven, and bake the turkey rolls for 30 minutes. Transfer the rolls to a platter and cover with aluminum foil; reserve the cooking juices.

To prepare the sauce

Combine the shallots, tarragon, and white wine and a pinch of pepper in a medium skillet over medium-high heat, bring to a low boil and reduce, stirring occasionally, until the wine is syrupy, about 5 minutes. Add the reserved cooking juices, stir to combine, and simmer for 1 minute. Meanwhile, combine the butter with the mustards in a small bowl and whisk to blend. Add the butter mixture a little at a time to the shallot mixture, whisking to incorporate. Keep warm over low heat until ready to serve.

To serve

Untie the turkey rolls cut into 1/2-inch slices. Place the sliced turkey rolls on each of 6 warmed serving plates, then drizzle with the mustard sauce. Serve warm with Macaroni Gratin.

[Magret de Canard à l'Orange]

Grilled Duck Breasts with Red Wine and Orange Sauce

Serves **6**

For the red wine and orange sauce

2 cups fresh orange juice
  (about 6 oranges)
1/2 cup honey
3 tablespoons sherry vinegar
4 cups dry red wine
2 cups chicken stock
2 tablespoons unsalted butter
2 teaspoons pumpkin pie spice mix,
  or use ground allspice

For the duck breasts

3 fresh magret duck breasts (about
  12 ounces each), skin on
2 tablespoons sunflower
  or vegetable oil
Freshly ground black pepper
Fine sea salt
4 tablespoons pumpkin pie spice
  mix, or use ground allspice

Duck breasts, called magrets, are a delicacy in France, to be enjoyed medium-rare, like a good steak. They're quick to cook, ready in about ten minutes. It's the sauce—here an intensely flavorful wine and orange juice reduction with honey, sherry vinegar, and spice—that takes a bit of time, about forty minutes, to achieve. Serve with Mille-feuilles of Crispy Potatoes (page 128), or sautéed potatoes.

To prepare the red wine and orange sauce

Combine the orange juice and honey in a large skillet and bring to a simmer over medium heat. Reduce, stirring frequently, until the mixture thickens to the consistency of a syrup, about 15 minutes. Add the vinegar, stir to combine, and cook for 2 minutes, stirring frequently. Add the wine, raise the heat to high, and cook, stirring frequently, until the mixture reduces by half, 8 to 10 minutes. Add the chicken stock and cook, stirring frequently, until the mixture reduces to a syrupy consistency, and there is about 1 1/2 cups of liquid remaining, 10 to 15 minutes. Remove the pan from the heat, add the quatre-épices or other spice mixture, season with salt and pepper to taste, and stir to incorporate. Add the butter and gently swirl with a wooden spoon until incorporated and the sauce takes on a satiny gloss. Keep the sauce warm over very low heat.

To prepare the duck breasts

Using a sharp knife, carefully remove about one-third of the fatty skin from the surface of each breast. With the tip of the knife, score the fat with a crosshatch design, being careful not to cut through to the meat. Spread the oil evenly over the duck breasts, then sprinkle them generously with salt and pepper. Sprinkle 2 teaspoons of the spice mix over each breast, a teaspoon on the fatty side and a teaspoon on the other side, and press the spices into the surfaces. Heat a large skillet over medium heat until hot. Place the duck breasts skin side down in the skillet, lower the heat just a notch to medium-low and cook for 7 to 8 minutes, until the skin is crisply browned. Spoon out excess fat from the pan as it is rendered. Turn the breasts and cook 3 to 4 minutes, until the meat on the opposite side is lightly browned. Transfer the breasts to a cutting board and set aside to rest for 5 minutes; they will continue to cook while resting.

Using a sharp carving knife, cut the duck breasts in half crosswise, then cut each half into 1/4-inch slices. Divide among six warmed serving plates, arranging the slices fat side up. Spoon the sauce over the duck and serve.

[Foie Gras Frais aux Pommes et aux Raisins]

Sautéed Fresh Foie Gras with Apples and Grapes

Serves **6**

For the port wine sauce

1 teaspoon canola oil

2 ounces raw foie gras, sliced
and reserved from 1-pound piece
(below), diced

2 Granny Smith apples, peeled,
quartered, seeded, and cut into
small chunks

1/4 pound seedless green grapes,
lightly pressed on a plate just
to break the skin

1/4 cup red port wine

1 teaspoon sherry vinegar

2 cups chicken stock

Fine sea salt

Freshly ground black pepper

For the fruit garnish

3 Granny Smith apples, peeled,
each cut into 6 wedges, seeded

2 tablespoons Clarified Butter
(see page 188)

8 red seedless grapes, halved

12 green seedless grapes, halved

Fine sea salt

Freshly ground black pepper

For the foie gras

1 1/2 pounds fresh foie gras, cleaned
of connective tissue and deveined;
let stand at room temperature
for 1 hour; slice off 2 ounces
(a very small morsel) and reserve
for the port wine sauce (above)

2 teaspoons canola oil

Fleur de sel, or coarse sea salt

Freshly ground black pepper

So lush, so luscious, such a splurge! There's nothing as opulent and sensuous as fresh sautéed foie gras, a dish perfectly accompanied by sautéed apples and grapes in a port wine sauce. Foie gras is somewhat difficult to work with, since it's so soft and buttery it almost melts in your hands. It should be at room temperature to slice, since it crumbles easily when it is chilled. It's easiest to cut with a very sharp knife heated in hot water, as explained below. Foie gras must be cooked very quickly, its cooking time counted in seconds, not minutes. The clarified butter (page 188), which takes only minutes, is important here; it makes the fruit garnish much more refined and flavorful. Serve with toasted slices of brioche, or challah with the crusts removed, in a pretty basket.

To prepare the port wine sauce

Heat the oil in a nonstick skillet pan over medium-high heat until very hot but not smoking. Brown the diced foie gras for 1 minute, stirring gently. Add the apples and sauté, stirring occasionally, for 2 minutes. Add the seedless grapes and sauté, stirring occasionally, for 1 minute. Add the port wine and cook, stirring occasionally, until the mixture reduces by half, about 3 minutes. Add the chicken stock, reduce the heat to medium, and cook, stirring occasionally, until the mixture thickens and reduces by half, 7 to 10 minutes. Add the vinegar, stir to combine, then strain the sauce into a medium saucepan through a fine-mesh strainer, or a colander lined with 3 layers of cheesecloth. Season to taste with salt and pepper and keep warm over very low heat.

To prepare the fruit garnish

Finely dice 6 of the apple wedges and set aside. Heat the clarified butter in a medium skillet over medium-high heat. Add the remaining 12 apple wedges and sauté, stirring occasionally, until the apples are golden brown, 5 to 7 minutes. Add the reserved diced apple and the red and green grape halves, stir to combine, and sauté 3 minutes. Season to taste with salt and pepper. Stir the apple mixture into the reserved port wine sauce, stir to combine, and keep warm over very low heat.

To prepare the foie gras

Before cutting the foie gras, prepare a pot of hot water to keep next to you for heating the knife. Using a very sharp knife, cut the foie gras crosswise into four 3/4- to 1-inch slices, dipping the knife into the hot water and drying it before each slice. Line a platter with paper towels and set aside. Heat 1 teaspoon of the oil in a nonstick skillet until the oil is very hot but not smoking. Add 2 slices of the foie gras and sear 45 to 60 seconds on each side, then transfer to the platter to drain. Wipe out the pan and repeat with the last 2 slices of foie gras.

Divide the foie gras slices among four warmed serving plates. Spoon the port wine sauce and the fruit next to the foie gras, sprinkle with a pinch of fleur de sel and pepper, and serve.

[Suprêmes de Volaille Pojarski]

Chicken Breasts Pojarski

Serves **6**

These delicious, chopped chicken patties—the base resembles a chicken meat loaf— are named, legend has it, for an eighteenth-century Russian innkeeper. The inside of the individual patties, best served sliced, is meltingly tender, while the exterior crust is golden and crunchy. The chicken mixture is sticky to work with, so it is chilled twice during preparation, once for one hour, so plan accordingly. The recipe calls for clarified butter, because the thick chicken patties must cook at least ten minutes over medium-high heat, and plain butter will burn. Remember to wash every part of your food processor thoroughly after chopping the raw chicken.

For the chicken Pojarski

8 ounces (about 8 pieces) dense,
   white sandwich bread,
   such as Arnold's Hearthstone,
   crusts trimmed, cubed
1 cup light cream
1 1/4 pounds skinless, boneless
   chicken breasts, coarsely chopped
   in a food processor
4 tablespoons (1/2 stick) unsalted
   butter, cut into bits, softened
1/4 teaspoon ground paprika
1/2 teaspoon fine sea salt
Freshly ground black pepper
3 large eggs
1 tablespoon extra-virgin olive oil
2 tablespoons whole milk or sour
   cream
1 tablespoon soy sauce
1 cup all-purpose flour
1 cup unflavored bread crumbs
Freshly ground black pepper
4 tablespoons Clarified Butter
   (see page 188)

For the parsley sauce

1 cup loosely packed coarsely
   chopped flat-leaf parsley leaves,
   stems removed
2 tablespoons chicken stock
Juice of 1/2 lemon
1 tablespoon extra-virgin olive oil

To prepare the chicken Pojarski

In a large mixing bowl, combine the cubed bread and the cream, stir to combine, then set aside for 20 minutes to allow the bread to absorb the cream. Return the mixture to the mixing bowl, add the chicken, 4 tablespoons of the butter, paprika, salt, and a dash of pepper and stir well with a wooden spoon to combine. Cover with plastic wrap and refrigerate for 20 minutes. Form the chicken mixture into 6 oval-shaped patties about 1 inch thick, place on a small baking sheet, cover with plastic wrap, and place in the freezer for 1 hour.

In a medium mixing bowl, combine the eggs, olive oil, milk, soy sauce, and several twists of freshly ground pepper and stir with a wooden spoon to combine. Place the flour on a dinner plate and the bread crumbs on a second dinner plate. Coat a chicken patty in flour, covering it well, then tapping it to remove excess flour. Dip the patty into the egg mixture, then immediately coat well with bread crumbs, and set on a small baking sheet. Repeat with the other 5 patties. Cover with plastic wrap and refrigerate for 10 or 15 minutes.

Meanwhile, prepare the parsley sauce

Bring a medium pot of water to boil. Fill a small bowl with cold water and several ice cubes. Place the parsley in a fine-mesh strainer and, holding the strainer over the pot, immerse the parsley into the boiling water for 5 seconds. Immediately dip the strainer into the bowl of ice water to chill the parsley. Drain the parsley, pat dry with paper towels, then transfer to the bowl of a small food processor and mince finely. Combine the parsley, chicken stock, lemon juice, a dash of salt and pepper, and the olive oil in a medium saucepan and heat slightly over medium-low heat for about 1 minute, whisking briskly to blend. Set aside in the pot.

In a large skillet over medium heat, melt the clarified butter. When the butter is bubbling, add the chicken patties and sauté, browning them on all sides. Continue sautéing until the patties are cooked through, about 10 minutes. (Since the patties are served sliced, you can cut into one to be sure the interior is completely cooked.)

Cut each patty into 1/3-inch slices, place the slices in the center of each serving plate, and drizzle with the parsley sauce. Serve, accompanied by Potatoes Boulangère (page 146) or whipped potatoes.

[Poulet en Fricassée]

Chicken Fricassee

Serves **6**

2 tablespoons olive oil

2 whole small chickens
(approximately 2 1/2 pounds each),
cut up into serving pieces

Freshly ground black pepper

8 tablespoons (1 stick)
unsalted butter

12 whole, unpeeled garlic cloves

1 1/2 cup aged, red wine vinegar

1 bouquet garni (2 sprigs tarragon,
1 sprig thyme, 1 bay leaf,
tied in a cheesecloth sachet)

Two 28-ounce cans crushed
tomatoes

2 tablespoons tomato paste

1/3 cup dry white wine

1 cup chicken stock

Fine sea salt

2 tablespoons chopped fresh
tarragon leaves for garnish

In a large cast-iron pot, heat the olive oil over high heat. (You may need to work in two batches so that the chicken can cook without crowding.) Add the chicken and a dash of salt and pepper. Stir the pieces to coat with the oil. When the chicken is partially browned, add the butter and the garlic cloves and stir to combine. Sauté, turning the chicken from time to time, until the chicken is deep golden brown, 12 to 14 minutes. Remove the chicken and garlic cloves, and pour out the grease from the pot. Reserve the garlic cloves. Return the chicken to the pot and set over medium-high heat. Add 1/4 cup of the vinegar to the pot, and stir to coat the chicken with the vinegar. Cook, stirring occasionally, until the vinegar becomes thick and syrupy, 3 to 4 minutes. Repeat 5 more times, adding 1/4 cup of vinegar at a time, until all the vinegar has been reduced to a syrup.

Add the bouquet garni, the reserved garlic cloves, crushed tomato, tomato paste, white wine, and chicken stock and stir to combine. Bring to a boil over high heat, then reduce the heat to medium-low, cover, and simmer for approximately 30 minutes, stirring occasionally.

Remove the chicken pieces from the sauce and keep warm on a platter in a low oven. Strain the sauce through a fine-mesh strainer back into the pot. Cook the sauce down over high heat until it reduces by about one-third and thickens, about 5 minutes. Season to taste. Divide the chicken among six warmed serving plates and bathe with the sauce. Garnish each serving with a pinch of chopped tarragon. Serve with baked macaroni or fresh tagliatelle.

[Poussin Rôti aux Gousses d'Ail]

Garlic-Roasted Cornish Hens with Cherry Sauce

Serves **6**

For the cherry sauce
(begin 24 hours in advance)

1 pound pitted dark sweet cherries, fresh or individually quick frozen, pitted
1 tablespoon sugar
1/2 cup cherry juice, or substitute cranberry juice
1/3 cup cider vinegarw
1 teaspoon fine sea salt

1 teaspoon fennel seeds
1 teaspoon red pepper flakes
1 strip lemon zest
2 slices bacon, cooked and crumbled

For the Cornish hens

6 tablespoons extra-virgin olive oil
Six 1 1/4- to 1 1/2-pound Cornish hens, livers reserved and legs trussed
12 unpeeled garlic cloves
3 branches fresh thyme
Fine sea salt
Freshly ground black pepper

For the liver spread (optional)

3 tablespoons unsalted butter
Reserved livers from the hens
Fine sea salt
Freshly ground black pepper
1/2 a long, thin French baguette, cut in 1/4-inch slices, toasted to light brown under the broiler

This recipe, originally created for squab, works beautifully with Cornish game hens. The liver spread is a delicious accompaniment to the bird, but is not essential to the recipe. Serve the hens with potatoes or a watercress salad with a lemony vinaigrette. Note: The cherry sauce must be started twenty-four hours ahead.

To prepare the cherry sauce (prepare 24 hours ahead)

Combine the cherries, sugar, cherry juice, cider vinegar, and salt in a medium bowl, and stir to dissolve the sugar and salt. Cover with aluminum foil or a plate, and refrigerate for 24 hours to allow the ingredients to macerate.

Preheat the oven to 300°F. Combine the fennel, pepper flakes, and lemon zest in a small bowl, stirring well. Transfer the mixture to a tea ball, or wrap in a small cheesecloth sachet and tie with string; set aside. Place half of the marinated cherry mixture in a food processor and purée. Combine the purée, whole cherries, marinade liquid, bacon, and the spice mixture in a medium ovenproof skillet or baking dish, cover, and bake for 1 hour, stirring occasionally. Set aside.

To prepare the hens

Preheat the oven to 375°F. Warm the olive oil over high heat in a large heavy-bottomed skillet. Working in batches, brown the hens on all sides, 5 to 7 minutes. Season with salt and pepper, transfer the hens to a large baking pan, or large baking sheet with 1-inch sides. Baste with the warm olive oil from the skillet. Scatter the garlic cloves and thyme around the birds and bake, basting occasionally, in the center of the oven for 40 to 45 minutes, until the birds are a deep golden brown and the juices run clear when the thigh is pierced, or until the internal temperature of the thigh reaches 170°F.

Meanwhile, prepare the liver spread

Melt 2 tablespoons of the butter in a large skillet over medium-high heat, add the livers, and stir to coat the livers well. Cook for 2 to 3 minutes, stirring frequently, until the livers are browned on all sides, then transfer to a medium bowl. Add the remaining 1 tablespoon of butter and mash well with a fork until smooth; season to taste with salt and pepper. Spread the warm mixture on slices of toasted baguette and set aside.

To serve

Place a hen on each of six serving plates. Scatter a few of the roasted garlic cloves on each plate, then spoon the cherry sauce around the hens. Garnish the plates with slices of toasted baguette with the liver spread, if you wish, and serve.

Vegetables

Provençal Stuffed Baby Vegetables

Cocotte of Winter Vegetables

Gratin of Fall Vegetables and Fruits

Pascal Vegetable Tartlets

Mille-feuilles of Crispy Potatoes

Octet of Stir-Fried Vegetables

Potato Gnocchi with Wild Mushrooms

Potato and Ham Gratin

Zucchini and Parmesan Risotto

Fresh Tagliatelle with Pesto and Mixed Vegetables

Penne Pasta with Tomato, Potato, and Onion

Creamy Polenta with Olives

Fricassee of Green Asparagus with Mushroom Ragout

Potatoes Boulangère

Celery Root with Chestnuts, Chanterelles, and Shallots

[Petits Farcis]

Serves **6**

For the vegetables

6 medium vine-ripened tomatoes

Fine sea salt

6 small round zucchini,
   or long zucchini

6 medium Yukon Gold potatoes

For the stuffing

3 tablespoons unsalted butter

2 tablespoon extra-virgin olive oil

3/4 pound boneless chicken breasts,
   cut into 2-inch chunks

Fine sea salt

Freshly ground black pepper

5 ounces smoked ham, cubed

3 shallots, chopped

2 garlic cloves, halved lengthwise

1/3 pound cremini or white
   mushrooms, stems trimmed,
   minced

2 tablespoons tomato paste

2 tablespoons finely chopped basil

For the assembly

6 tablespoons unsalted butter,
   plus butter for the baking dish

4 tablespoons extra-virgin olive oil,
   plus more for garnish

2 cups chicken stock

Fleur de sel, or coarse sea salt

Freshly ground black pepper

6 sprigs flat-leaf parsley for garnish

These plump, appetizing little stuffed vegetables require a bit of time and effort in preparation, but are extremely tasty and very versatile. You can serve them warm or cold, as a starter or as a main course, or on a buffet table.

To prepare the **tomatoes**

Slice 1/2 inch from the top of the tomatoes to create a small cap; do not remove the stem. Scoop out the seeds and flesh; discard the seeds, reserve the flesh. Sprinkle the cavities with salt, place upside down on a wire rack set over a platter or baking sheet to catch the drips, and drain for 30 minutes. Chop the reserved flesh and set aside.

To prepare the **zucchini**

Cut a small slice from the bottom of the zucchini so that it will sit upright. For a round zucchini: Slice off the top 1/4 of the zucchini to make a "cap;" do not remove the stem. For a long zucchini: Lay in a horizontal position and slice off the top 1/4 of the zucchini to make a "cap," starting 1 inch from the end and stopping 1 inch from the other end. Bring a large pot of salted water to a boil, add the zucchini and blanch for 1 minute, then rinse under cold running water. Scoop out the centers, leaving enough flesh to ensure a firm shell. Finely chop the interior flesh and reserve with the shells.

To prepare the **potatoes**

Lay the potatoes in a horizontal position and slice off about 1/4 of the upper part to make a "cap." Carefully carve out the center of the potatoes, leaving enough flesh to maintain a firm shell. Finely chop the interior flesh and reserve with the shells.

To prepare the **stuffing**

Combine 1 tablespoon of the butter and 1 tablespoon of olive oil in a medium skillet. When the butter is bubbling, add the chicken, season with salt and pepper, and sauté, stirring occasionally, until the chicken is lightly browned on all sides but not cooked through, about 3 minutes. Combine the chicken and the ham in the bowl of a food processor, or in a meat grinder, and pulse or grind until finely chopped. Set aside. Melt the remaining 2 tablespoons of butter with the remaining 1 tablespoon of olive oil in a medium skillet over medium heat. Add the shallots, garlic, and mushrooms and sauté, stirring frequently, until the liquid has evaporated, about 5 minutes. Combine the chicken mixture, mushroom mixture, tomato paste, basil, and reserved vegetable flesh in a large bowl. Season with salt and pepper, and stir well to incorporate.

To assemble and serve

Preheat the oven to 300°F. Fill the vegetables with the stuffing, mounding it slightly above the tops. Top each with 1 teaspoon of butter, place the "caps" on, and arrange in two buttered gratin dishes or baking pans at least 2 inches deep. Drizzle each with 1 teaspoon of olive oil. Add 1 cup of chicken stock to each gratin dish and cover with aluminum foil. Bake for 1 hour, basting halfway through. Remove the foil after 45 minutes. Divide the vegetables among six warmed serving plates, and drizzle with some of the cooking liquid, plus a few drops of olive oil, if you wish. Sprinkle with fleur de sel and pepper, garnish with a sprig of parsley, and serve immediately.

[Légumes d'Hiver en Cocotte]

Cocotte of Winter Vegetables

Serves 6

8 tablespoons (1 stick) unsalted
 butter
2 Bartlett or Comice pears, peeled,
 cored, and quartered
10 unpeeled garlic cloves
1/2 cup plus 3 tablespoons
 extra-virgin olive oil
6 carrots, peeled and coarsely
 chopped
3 turnips, peeled and coarsely
 chopped
6 new potatoes, peeled
 and quartered
1/2 cup chicken stock
1 white onion, peeled and quartered
1/2 green cabbage, cored,
 cut into quarters
9 green asparagus, trimmed
 and cut in half crosswise
6 mushrooms, trimmed
 and cut in half lengthwise
Freshly ground black pepper
18 whole roasted chestnuts
 (fresh, canned, or frozen;
 not packed in syrup)
1/3 pound slab bacon, cut into
 1-inch-long matchstick strips
6 tfrozen or canned artichoke hearts,
 thawed or drained, sliced
Fine sea salt

This richly flavored vegetable dish, savory with root vegetables and bacon, would make a nice main course, or a delicious side dish to a Sunday roast. To add a dash of fresh, sweet crunch in contrast to the cooked vegetables, you can garnish each serving with shavings of tart apple or crisp raw pear.

In a medium skillet over medium-high heat, melt 2 tablespoons of butter, add the pears and stir to combine. Cook, stirring frequently, until the pears turn golden, about 5 minutes. Set aside.

In a small saucepan, combine the garlic cloves and 1/2 cup olive oil. Set over low heat and cook, stirring frequently, until soft, about 20 minutes. Separate the peels from the garlic and discard the peels. Set the garlic aside.

Blanch the carrots and turnips for 30 seconds in boiling salted water. Drain and set aside.

In a large stockpot, melt 4 tablespoons of the butter and 3 tablespoons of olive oil over medium-high heat. Add the potatoes and cook for 5 minutes, stirring frequently. Add the carrots and turnips and cook for 10 minutes, stirring frequently. Add the chicken stock, onion, cabbage, asparagus, and mushrooms and stir to combine. Season with salt and pepper and cook for another 10 minutes, stirring occasionally. Set aside.

In a medium skillet, melt the remaining 2 tablespoons of butter over medium-high heat. Add the bacon and cook, stirring frequently, for 2 minutes. Add the chestnuts and artichokes and cook, stirring frequently for 5 minutes. Add the chestnut mixture, the reserved garlic, and reserved pears to the vegetable mixture. Mix gently to combine, season with salt and pepper, and serve immediately.

[Légumes et Fruits d'Automne au Gratin]

Gratin of Fall Vegetables and Fruits

Serves 10

6 potatoes, peeled and cut
  into 1/8-inch slices
1/2 pound fresh pumpkin, peeled and
  sliced into 1/2-inch cubes
Fine sea salt
Freshly ground black pepper
4 tablespoons unsalted butter
4 tablespoons extra-virgin olive oil
1 1/4 cups chicken stock
6 canned or frozen artichoke hearts
2 Anjou or Comice pears, peeled and
  cored, each cut lengthwise into
  8 slices
1/2 pound wild or cultivated
  mushrooms, such as chanterelles,
  shiitake, or cremini
1 garlic clove, peeled and finely
  chopped

For a winning accompaniment to a roast breast of veal, pork loin, or roast turkey, you couldn't do better than this tasty fall fruit and vegetable side dish. It would make a lovely addition to the Thanksgiving table. The recipe is a bit labor-intensive, since each component must be prepared separately. Plan on thirty minutes of prep time, followed by one hour and fifteen minutes of cooking time. For extra texture and sweetness, you could toss in a handful of seedless red grapes when you assemble the fruits and vegetables in the baking dish.

Place 2 tablespoons of the butter and 1 tablespoon of the olive oil into a large skillet and melt over high heat. Cook the potatoes in batches, stirring occasionally, until golden around the edges. Season each batch with salt and pepper, transfer to a bowl, and set aside.

Heat 1 tablespoon of the olive oil in the skillet and cook the cubed pumpkin over medium-high heat until golden. Add 1/4 cup of the chicken stock and cook, stirring occasionally, for 5 minutes. Transfer to a bowl and set aside.

Heat the skillet over medium-high heat, then add 1 tablespoon of olive oil. Once the olive oil is warm, add the artichoke hearts and cook for 2 minutes, stirring occasionally. Add 1/4 cup of the chicken stock, stir to combine, cover, and cook for 5 more minutes. Set aside to cool. Once cooled, cut each artichoke into 3 slices. Season with salt and pepper, transfer to a bowl, and set aside.

Place 2 tablespoons of butter into a large skillet over medium heat. Add the sliced pears and cook until slightly golden, about 3 minutes per side. Transfer to a bowl and set aside.

Remove the woody stems from the mushrooms and wash them under cold water. Slice them into 3 or 4 slices, depending on size. In a large skillet over high heat, add 1 tablespoon of olive oil. Once the pan is hot, add the mushrooms and cook, stirring occasionally, 3 to 4 minutes, until the mushrooms begin to release their liquid. Add the garlic and a pinch of salt and stir to combine. Cook for 1 minute, stirring occasionally, and set aside in the skillet.

Preheat the oven to 350°F. Butter a 9 by 9-inch gratin or baking dish, and add the vegetables and fruit in layers: potatoes, pumpkin, artichokes, pears, and mushrooms. Pour the remaining 3/4 cup chicken stock over the layers, and bake the gratin for 30 minutes, until the mixture is bubbling and the top is browned. Serve immediately.

[Tourte Pascaline aux Légumes]

Pascal Vegetable Tartlets

Serves **6**

1 1/2 cups frozen baby peas, thawed

1 cup frozen lima beans, thawed

2 medium zucchini, sliced into thin ribbons with a vegetable peeler

1/4 pound fresh spinach, stems trimmed, sliced into strips

2 frozen or canned artichoke hearts, thawed or drained, sliced

3 small white onions, minced

3 large eggs

1/4 cup grated Reggiano Parmesan cheese, or other good Parmesan

9 tablespoons extra-virgin olive oil

One 17-ounce package commercial puff pastry

Fine sea salt

Freshly ground black pepper

1 large egg beaten with 1 tablespoon water, for the glaze

In French cooking, a tourte is a covered tart like an American double-crusted pie. The recipe here is named for an old-fashioned Easter tart that features a whole cooked egg in the center of the filling. The egg, of course, is a symbol of Easter, of rebirth, of life. In this version of the Pascal Torte, beaten eggs combine with six vegetables to form the filling of individual tartlets capped with little pastry lids. To prepare the tourte in the traditional way, as one large 9-inch pie with a top crust, follow the directions in the Note at the end of this recipe.

Combine the peas, beans, zucchini, spinach, artichoke, and onions in a large bowl, and stir to mix well. Combine the eggs, Parmesan, and 6 tablespoons of olive oil in a small bowl, and whisk to blend. Pour the egg mixture into the vegetable mixture and stir to combine. Season generously with salt and pepper, and set aside.

Preheat the oven to 375°F. On a floured work surface, using a floured rolling pin, roll out the two pastry sheets into 1/8-inch-thick rectangles. Using a 5-inch biscuit cutter or an inverted 5-inch bowl as a guide, cut out six 5-inch circles from the pastry dough. Reserve the remaining dough. Press the pastry circles gently into the bottoms and sides of six buttered, 4-inch, removable-bottom tart pans, then prick the bottoms of the crusts several times with the tines of a fork, and set aside. Gather and roll out again the remaining dough. Using a cookie cutter or a small cup as a guide, cut out six 3 1/2-inch circles from the dough; these will be the lids for the tartlets. Score the top of the lids in the shape of a circle 1/2 inch in from the edges, being careful not to cut through the dough. Score a delicate crosshatch design around the edges. Set aside.

Divide the filling among the 6 tartlet shells. Brush the rims of the tartlets, and the tops of the 6 pastry lids, with the remaining olive oil. Place the tartlets on one baking sheet and the pastry lids on a second baking sheet. Place the tartlets on the top rack of the oven and the pastry lids on the rack below. Bake the pastry lids for about 18 minutes, until they are golden brown; set aside on a wire rack to cool. Bake the tartlets for 30 to 35 minutes, until the pastry is nicely browned and the filling firm. Transfer the tartlets to a wire rack and cool for 10 minutes. Serve the tartlets warm, topped with their pastry lids.

Note: To make this tourte as one large pie, roll the dough as stated above. Cut out two 10-inch circles from the pastry dough. Fill the tart pan with one of the pastry circles, spoon in the filling and top with the second pastry circle, pressing or crimping the edges to seal. Cut a 3/4-inch hole in the center of the top pastry circle; this is a little vent that allows steam to escape during baking. Bake 40 to 45 minutes, then transfer to a wire rack to cool for 10 minutes. Serve warm.

Mille-feuilles
of Crispy Potatoes

Serves **6**

3 large russet potatoes, peeled
  and thinly sliced

2 cups peanut or vegetable oil

3/4 pound frozen fava or baby lima
  beans

2 tablespoons extra-virgin olive oil

1 garlic clove, unpeeled

6 frozen or canned artichoke hearts,
  thawed or drained, sliced in
  eighths

3 tablespoons sherry vinegar

2/3 cup chicken stock

24 pieces Tomato Confit
  (see page 186), or sun-dried
  tomatoes in oil, drained and sliced
  into strips

4 fresh chives, cut into 1/2-inch
  pieces

10 fresh basil leaves, coarsely
  chopped

Fine sea salt

Freshly ground black pepper

6 cherry tomatoes, halved crosswise

Fleur de sel, or coarse sea salt

The term "mille-feuilles" literally translated means "a thousand leaves" or "a thousand layers." Mille-feuilles are traditionally layered pastries, but the term has been popularized in restaurants describing any kind of multi-layered dish. This potato and vegetable composition is elegant on the plate and marvelously flavorful. You will need six 3- or 4-inch pastry rings or biscuit cutters. The mille-feuilles are best when prepared just before serving. Serve as a first course or as a side dish to a roast lamb or beef.

Submerge the potato rounds in a large bowl of cold water to remove the starch. Drain and dry them completely with paper towels. Heat the peanut oil in a large skillet over medium-high heat. When hot (330°F), cook the potato slices in batches until golden brown, about 7 minutes per batch. Place on paper towels to drain, and keep warm until ready to use.

Cook the beans in boiling salted water until soft, about 5 minutes. Drain and set aside. In a medium saucepan over medium-high heat, add the olive oil and garlic and sauté, stirring frequently, for 30 seconds. Add the artichokes and cook for 3 minutes. Remove the garlic clove and add the vinegar. Continue to cook until the liquid evaporates, about 3 minutes, stirring frequently. Add the chicken stock, reduce the heat to low, and simmer for 5 minutes more. Add the tomato confit, reserved beans, chives, and all but 2 tablespoons of the basil. Stir well and cook until the mixture is warmed through, about 5 minutes. Season to taste with salt and pepper.

Place a pastry ring on each serving plate and fan 3 slices of potato to create a bottom layer inside the pastry ring. Add 2 to 3 tablespoons of filling and top with a second fan of potatoes. Repeat once more, finishing with another potato fan. Carefully slide the pastry rings up and off. Garnish each mille-feuilles with the top half of a cherry tomato (reserve the bottoms for another use), sprinkle with pinches of the remaining basil and fleur de sel, and serve.

[Légumes au Wok]

Octet of Stir-Fried Vegetables

Serves 6

3 tablespoons extra-virgin olive oil
2 garlic cloves, crushed
4 carrots, peeled and thinly sliced
   lengthwise
3 small zucchini, peeled and thinly
   sliced lengthwise
1/4 head cauliflower, coarsely
   chopped
6 frozen or canned artichoke hearts,
   thawed or drained, sliced
2 celery stalks, leaves trimmed,
   cut into 1/2-inch pieces
1/3 pound fresh or frozen snow peas
6 ounces romaine lettuce,
   cut into strips
3 or 4 stalks Swiss chard,
   cut into strips
1 cup soybeans
1/4 cup soy sauce
Freshly ground pepper

Vibrant, healthy, and easy to prepare, this eight-vegetable combo makes a lovely light dinner served with steamed rice, or a great side dish for tuna or other fish. For additional crunch, you can toss in a handful of fresh, raw baby spinach or a cup of chopped, raw endives just before serving.

In a large stockpot over medium-high heat, warm the olive oil and garlic. Add the carrots, zucchini, cauliflower, artichoke, celery, snow peas, lettuce, Swiss chard, and soybeans. Sprinkle with pepper. Cook, covered, for approximately 7 minutes, or until the vegetables begin to soften, stirring occasionally. Add the soy sauce and continue to cook for an additional 5 minutes, stirring occasionally. Season to taste and serve warm.

[Gnocchi de Pommes de Terre et Cèpes]

Potato Gnocchi with Wild Mushrooms

Serves **4**

For the mushrooms

1 tablespoon duck fat, or unsalted butter

1 pound porcini or cremini mushrooms, cleaned, stems trimmed, and halved

5 ounces slab bacon, diced

2 garlic cloves, unpeeled

2 sprigs thyme

1 1/4 cups veal or chicken stock

Fine sea salt

Freshly ground black pepper

For the gnocchi

1 pound packaged gnocchi

3 tablespoons unsalted butter, cut into bits

2 tablespoons chopped flat-leaf parsley

1/4 pound Reggiano Parmesan cheese, or other good Parmesan, shaved into curls

Fleur de sel, or coarse sea salt

Quick and delicious, this recipe, which calls for packaged gnocchi, is ready in just twenty minutes.

To prepare the mushrooms

In a large skillet, melt the duck fat over medium-high heat. Add the mushrooms, bacon, garlic, and thyme and sauté, stirring frequently, until the mushrooms soften and begin to release their juices and the bacon is slightly browned, about 5 minutes. Add the stock, reduce the heat to low, and simmer the mixture for 10 minutes, stirring occasionally. Remove the thyme sprigs and garlic, and season the mixture to taste with salt and pepper. Keep warm in a low oven until ready to use.

To prepare the gnocchi

Cook the gnocchi in boiling, salted water according to the package instructions. (Normally, you cook gnocchi very briefly, just until they float to the surface of the water.) Using a large slotted spoon, transfer the gnocchi to a wide, buttered bowl. Add the gnocchi and the butter to the warm mushroom mixture and stir gently to combine. Taste and adjust the seasoning if necessary. Spoon the gnocchi mixture into warmed soup bowls, garnish with chopped parsley, Parmesan curls, and a sprinkle of fleur de sel, and serve immediately.

[Gratin Boulangère]

Potato and Ham Gratin

Serves **6**

4 tablespoons (1 stick) unsalted
  butter
3 medium onions, peeled,
  thinly sliced
Fine sea salt
Freshly ground black pepper
6 slices of cured Serrano or
  prosciutto ham, sliced in thin
  strips
2 pounds large Yukon Gold potatoes,
  peeled and thinly sliced
20 pieces Tomato Confit
  (see page 186), or use sun-dried
  tomatoes in oil, drained and
  coarsely chopped
3 cups chicken stock

This flavorful gratin makes a savory side dish for a roast beef or leg of lamb. To make this dish even richer and more luscious, substitute 1/2 cup of heavy cream for 1/2 cup of the chicken stock.

In a large skillet, melt the butter over medium-high heat, add the onions and stir to combine. Reduce the heat to low and cook, covered, for 40 minutes, stirring occasionally, until the onions are soft and lightly caramelized. Season with salt and pepper. Add the ham and stir to combine.

Preheat the oven to 350°F. In a large (13 by 9-inch) buttered baking dish, arrange the potatoes in three layers, overlapping the slices in each layer and sprinkling salt and pepper over the top of each layer. Spread the onion mixture over the top of the potatoes, then top with the tomatoes. Pour the chicken stock over the tomatoes, and cover the dish with aluminum foil. Bake for 45 minutes, remove the foil top, and bake for 25 to 30 minutes more, or until the potatoes are cooked through and the top is golden brown. Serve warm.

[Risotto aux Courgettes et Parmesan]

Zucchini and Parmesan Risotto

Serves 6

5 cups chicken stock
4 tablespoons extra-virgin olive oil
4 small white onions, finely chopped
1 1/2 cups Arborio, or other short-
   grain round or semi-round rice
1/2 cup dry white wine
3 small zucchini, diced
3 tablespoons salted butter
1 cup freshly grated Reggiano
   Parmesan cheese, or other
   imported Parmesan
5 basil leaves, finely sliced
Fleur de sel, or coarse sea salt
1/4 pound piece of Reggiano
   Parmesan cheese, or other imported
   Parmesan, sliced in thin slivers

This is a luscious and easy-to-prepare risotto, perfect either as an appetizer or a main course. Using a premium European demi-sel or "half-salted" butter, such as the Danish Lurpak or a French butter from Brittany, will make this dish even more delicious, as will a fine chicken stock. Using top-quality ingredients is very important to a good risotto.

In a large saucepan over high heat, bring the chicken stock to a full boil, then turn off the heat and set the stock aside. In a large pot, warm the olive oil over medium heat. When the pot is warm, add the onions, reduce the heat to low, and cook, stirring frequently, until the onions are translucent, 15 to 20 minutes; do not allow the onions to brown or they will turn bitter. Increase the heat to medium-high and add the rice. Stir constantly for 2 to 3 minutes until the rice is well coated with the olive oil and begins to turn translucent. Add the white wine, stir to combine, then cook, stirring occasionally, until the wine evaporates completely, 2 to 3 minutes. Add enough chicken stock to just cover the rice. Cook, stirring frequently, until the rice absorbs the liquid, about 7 minutes. Add the remaining stock and continue to cook, stirring frequently, for another 10 minutes. Add the diced zucchini and stir to combine. Continue cooking, stirring frequently, 9 to 10 minutes, until the rice is fully cooked and has formed a creamy sauce. Remove from the heat, add the butter, Parmesan, and basil, and stir to combine. Taste and adjust the seasoning as necessary. Divide the risotto among heated serving plates, sprinkle with the basil, a pinch of fleur de sel, and Parmesan slivers, and serve immediately.

[Pâtes Fraîches au Pistou]

Fresh Tagliatelle with Pesto and Mixed Vegetables

Serves **6** *to* **8**

For the mixed vegetables

4 tablespoons extra-virgin olive oil

2 slim young carrots, peeled
  and thinly sliced

3 small young turnips, peeled
  and thinly sliced

3 frozen artichoke hearts, thawed,
  thinly sliced

2 small, slim zucchini, finely
  chopped

I small fennel bulb, leaves trimmed,
  finely chopped

3 white onions, finely chopped

1/2 cup fresh peas, or thawed,
  frozen peas

1/2 cup fresh or frozen fava
  or baby lima beans

6 ripe plum tomatoes, peeled,
  seeded, and sliced into 8 wedges

Fine sea salt

Freshly ground pepper

For the pesto

I cup frozen fava or baby lima beans

I bunch basil, stems removed

Fine sea salt

I cup extra-virgin olive oil

For the pasta

2 quarts chicken stock

I pound fresh tagliatelle pasta

Coarse sea salt

This is a pesto with a difference—one prepared with basil and fava or baby lima beans instead of the traditional pine nuts. Nine different vegetables comprise the sumptuous garnish, so that the dish makes a generous main course for six or more. On a night when you want to prepare a quick-and-easy dish, you can serve the tagliatelle topped only with the pesto sauce—simply delicious. The pasta and sauce on their own (without the vegetables) will serve 4.

To prepare the mixed vegetables

In a large pot, heat the olive oil. Once warm, add the carrots, turnips, artichokes, zucchini, fennel, onions, peas, and fava beans into the pot and sauté for 10 minutes, until the vegetables are slightly softened, but not browned. Stir occasionally. Add the tomato wedges and cook for 2 minutes more. Season with salt and pepper and set aside.

To prepare the pesto

Cook the fava beans in boiling salted water until warm, about 4 minutes. Drain. Place the beans, basil, and a pinch of salt in the bowl of a food processor. Purée on high until a paste forms, about I minute. While the food processor is running, pour in the olive oil in a slow, steady stream until combined. Taste and adjust the seasoning.

To prepare the pasta

In a large pot, bring the stock to a boil and cook the pasta according to the package instructions, then drain. Place the vegetable garnish in the center of the serving plates and place the pasta on top. Drizzle with the pesto and sprinkle with a pinch of coarse sea salt. Serve warm.

Vegetables

[Pâtes Façon Moulinier]

Penne Pasta with Tomato, Potato, and Onion

Serves **6**

6 cups chicken stock

6 tablespoons extra-virgin olive oil

6 new potatoes, peeled and thinly sliced

3 plum tomatoes, peeled, quartered, and seeded

2 white onions, minced

2 garlic cloves, peeled and crushed

1/2 bunch basil, leaves coarsely chopped, stems reserved

Fine sea salt

Freshly ground pepper

1 pound penne pasta

1/2 cup grated Reggiano Parmesan cheese, or other good Parmesan

In a large saucepan, bring the chicken stock to a boil, turn off the heat, and set aside. In a large stockpot, heat 4 tablespoons of the olive oil over medium-high heat. Add the potatoes, tomatoes, onions, garlic, and basil stems. Season with salt and pepper, and stir well. Add the pasta to the vegetables and stir to combine. Pour half of the chicken stock onto the vegetable-pasta mixture and cook until all the liquid has evaporated, approximately 10 minutes. Stir occasionally, scraping the bottom to loosen any ingredients that may be stuck. Add the remaining chicken stock and continue to cook until the liquid evaporates, approximately 15 minutes more, stirring occasionally. Remove and discard the basil stems, add the remaining 2 tablespoons of olive oil, half of the chopped basil leaves, and the Parmesan and stir to combine. Divide the pasta among six warmed serving bowls, garnish with the remaining basil leaves, and serve.

Vegetables

[Polenta Moelleuse aux Olives]

Creamy Polenta with Olives

Serves **6**

For the olive garnish

1/2 pound (about 30) pitted black
    and/or green brine-cured olives,
    such as Picholine, Kalamata,
    or Niçoise
1 tablespoon extra-virgin olive oil
1 tablespoon unsalted butter
1/4 pound slab bacon, diced
6 cloves Garlic Confit (see page 187),
    or 3 cloves garlic, lightly crushed,
    cut in half
1/2 cup chicken stock
2 tablespoons chopped fresh rosemary
Freshly ground black pepper

For the polenta

1 cup (8 ounces) quick-cooking
    polenta (also called instant polenta
    or precooked cornmeal)
4 tablespoons unsalted butter
1 tablespoon extra-virgin olive oil
Fine sea salt
3/4 cup mascarpone cheese
1 cup grated Reggiano Parmesan,
    or other good Parmesan cheese
Freshly ground black pepper
6 small sprigs rosemary
Reggiano Parmesan cheese shavings,
    optional for garnish

This polenta, topped with a savory mix of olives, bacon and garlic, is a terrific accompaniment to all kinds of veal dishes, such as the Veal Medallions with Tomato Sauce on page 98, as well as to a variety of tuna preparations, such as the Bay of Biscay Tuna Fillet on page 78. Part of this polenta's appeal is its neat, carefully molded round shape. The ideal tool for achieving this presentation is a 4-inch pastry ring. You can also use a 3 1/2- to 4-inch ramekin. Even an individual 1-cup measure will work.

To prepare the olive garnish

Blanch the olives for 3 minutes in a small pot of boiling water. Drain and set aside. Heat the olive oil and the butter in a medium skillet over medium-high heat. Add the bacon and the garlic cloves, reduce the heat to medium-low, and sauté, stirring occasionally, until the bacon starts to brown slightly and the garlic softens, about 3 minutes. Add the chicken stock and the chopped rosemary, raise the heat to medium-high, and cook, stirring occasionally, until the liquid reduces by half, about 6 minutes. Remove the garlic cloves and reserve. Add the reserved, drained olives and a generous pinch of pepper, stir to combine, then keep warm in a low oven.

To prepare the polenta

Combine 5 cups of water, 1 tablespoon of the butter, 1 tablespoon of olive oil, and 1 teaspoon of salt in a large pot, and bring to a boil over high heat. Pour the polenta into the pot in a thin stream, stirring constantly with a large spoon. Reduce the heat to low and cook, stirring continuously, to keep the polenta smooth, 4 to 5 minutes, until the polenta thickens. Remove from the heat, add the remaining 3 tablespoons butter, mascarpone, and the Reggiano Parmesan cheese, and stir to incorporate. The polenta should be soft and unctuous. Season with salt and pepper to taste.

To assemble and serve

*If using 4-inch pastry rings: Place a pastry ring in the center of each serving dish. Spoon the polenta into the rings, filling almost to the top. Carefully remove the pastry rings. *If using 3 1/2- to 4-inch ramekins: Lightly grease the ramekins with olive oil. Fill the ramekins with the polenta, pressing the polenta gently with the back of a spoon to be flush with the sides of the ramekin. Reverse the ramekins onto six serving dishes, shaking slightly if necessary to release the molded polenta. Make a small indentation in the center of each molded polenta, and fill with a heaping tablespoon of the olive garnish. Decorate with rosemary sprigs, the reserved garlic cloves, and Parmesan shavings, if you wish, and serve.

[Fricassée d'Asperges Vertes]

Fricassee of Green Asparagus with Mushroom Ragout

Serves **6**

Fine sea salt

30 stalks fresh green asparagus, trimmed 5 inches from the tips and peeled

6 tablespoon unsalted butter

2 medium shallots, minced

2 garlic cloves, finely chopped

10 ounces small white or cremini mushrooms, stems trimmed, sliced into quarters

Freshly ground black pepper

1 1/2 cup chicken stock

3/4 cup grated Reggiano Parmesan cheese, or other good Parmesan

Mushrooms and asparagus famously star together in risottos and other pasta favorites such as fettuccine or farfalle. Here, in this vegetable fricassee, they go it alone with great success. The mushrooms cook into a flavorful ragout that tops the buttered asparagus. A sprinkling of Reggiano Parmesan cheese adds a rich, nutty note to the ensemble. Serve with a roast beef, lamb, or grilled chicken.

Bring a pot of salted water to a boil, add the asparagus, and cook 5 to 7 minutes, until just tender. Gently transfer to a platter with tongs, avoiding the fragile tips, pat dry with paper towels, and set aside.

Melt 3 tablespoon of the butter in a large skillet over medium-low heat. Add the shallots and sauté, stirring frequently, for 2 minutes. Add the garlic and sauté, stirring frequently, for 2 minutes. Add the mushrooms and a generous pinch of salt and pepper and sauté, stirring occasionally, for 3 minutes. Raise the heat to medium, add the chicken stock, and simmer, stirring occasionally, for 15 minutes. Using a slotted spoon, transfer the mushroom to a bowl and set aside. Raise the heat to high and boil, stirring occasionally, until the sauce reduces to about 3/4 cup. Pour the sauce into the mushrooms, stir to combine, and keep warm in a low oven.

Melt the remaining 3 tablespoons of the butter in a large skillet over medium heat. Add the asparagus in a single layer and shake the pan gently to coat the stalks with the melted butter. Sprinkle with the grated cheese. Remove the pan from the heat and allow the asparagus to remain in the pan for 2 minutes so the cheese can melt slightly. Arrange the asparagus side by side on a warmed platter. Spoon the mushroom ragout across the center of the asparagus and serve.

[Pommes Boulangère]

Potatoes Boulangère

Serves **6**

For the potatoes

18 small new potatoes, peeled
Fine sea salt
6 tablespoons unsalted butter
2 unpeeled garlic cloves
1 cup chicken stock
Freshly ground black pepper

For the onion marmalade

1 tablespoon extra-virgin olive oil
1/4 pound slab bacon,
   cut into matchstick strips about
   1 inch long and 1/4 inch wide
1 tablespoon unsalted butter
12 small new white onions,
   peeled and minced
3/4 cup chicken stock
Fine sea salt
Freshly ground black pepper

These are sautéed potatoes with a little twist—a savory onion "marmalade" topping. It's not a true marmalade, of course, but after the onions cook down slowly with a bit of bacon, the texture of the mixture is reminiscent of a fruit marmalade.

To prepare the potatoes

Bring a large pot of salted water to a boil over high heat. Add the potatoes and cook for 20 minutes, until just tender, then drain. In a large skillet, melt 5 tablespoons of the butter over medium heat, add the garlic cloves, and stir to combine. Cook, stirring frequently, for 1 minute. Add the potatoes and a pinch of fine sea salt and pepper and stir to combine. Sauté, stirring frequently, until the potatoes are well browned, about 15 minutes. Add the remaining tablespoon of butter and the chicken stock and stir to combine. Cook, stirring often, until the potatoes are very tender, 10 to 15 minutes. Keep warm in a low oven.

To prepare the onion marmalade

Heat the olive oil in a medium skillet over medium heat. Add the bacon and sauté, stirring often, until the bacon is browned, about 5 minutes. Spoon out and discard the excess fat. Add the butter and stir to combine. When the butter has melted, add the onions and stir to combine. Sauté, stirring frequently, for 3 minutes, just until the onions begin to turn translucent. Add the chicken stock, a generous pinch of salt, and several twists of the pepper mill, and stir to combine. Reduce heat to medium-low and simmer, stirring frequently, until the onions are very soft and the stock has reduced to about 1/3 cup. Serve the potatoes, about 3 per person, as a side dish topped with 2 to 3 tablespoons of the onion "marmalade."

[Céleri-Rave aux Échalotes]

Celery Root with Chestnuts, Chanterelles, and Shallots

Serves **6**

2 cups kosher salt, for baking

12 long shallots, unpeeled

8 tablespoons (1 stick) unsalted butter

1 large head (about 1 1/4 pounds) celery root, peeled, cut into 1/2-inch rounds, then into 1/2-inch-wide strips

3 ounces slab bacon, sliced into matchstick strips

18 whole roasted chestnuts, in a jar or canned

Fine sea salt

Freshly ground black pepper

1/2 cup chicken stock

1/4 pound chanterelle mushrooms, or substitute 1/2 pound cremini mushrooms, cleaned thoroughly, dried, stems removed

2 tablespoons chopped flat-leaf parsley

Earthy from the celery root, shallots, and chanterelle mushrooms, and with a touch of sweetness from the chestnuts, this fragrant, delectable vegetable side dish would be perfect for a winter holiday table. Serve it with roast turkey, a crown roast of pork, or a plump roast goose. You can substitute cremini mushrooms for the usually high-priced chanterelle mushrooms. Clean the mushrooms very carefully, in all the little crevices, with a soft brush. Use as little water as possible, especially with the delicate chanterelles. Never soak mushrooms—they quickly become waterlogged.

Preheat the oven to 200°F. Place the kosher salt in a small casserole and lay the shallots over the top. Cover, place in the center of the oven, and bake for 1 1/2 to 2 hours. Set aside, covered, to cool.

In a large skillet, melt 4 tablespoons of the butter over medium heat. Add the celery root strips, and toss to coat with butter. Cover, reduce the heat to medium and cook, stirring occasionally, until the celery root has softened and is lightly browned, about 10 minutes. Transfer to a bowl and keep warm in the oven on very low heat.

In a large skillet, melt 2 tablespoons of the butter over medium heat. Add the bacon and sauté, stirring frequently, until the bacon has browned, about 4 minutes. Stir in the chestnuts, season with salt and pepper, and sauté, stirring occasionally, for 2 minutes. Add the chicken stock, raise the heat to high, and bring to a boil. Reduce the heat to medium and simmer, stirring occasionally, for 5 minutes. Transfer the mixture to the bowl with the celery root and keep warm in the oven on very low heat.

Return the pan to medium heat, add the remaining 2 tablespoons of butter and melt. When the butter is bubbling, add the chanterelle mushrooms and sauté, stirring frequently, just until the mushrooms begin to release their juices, about 3 minutes. Season with salt and pepper, sprinkle with chopped parsley, and remove from the heat. Add the mushrooms to the bowl with the celery-root mixture, and stir gently to combine. Arrange the celery-root mixture on a warmed serving platter. Slice the shallots (still in their skin) in half lengthwise and arrange decoratively around the border. Serve immediately.

Desserts

Butter-Rum Bananas with Chocolate Sauce and Vanilla Ice Cream

Cherry Vacherin

Sauternes Fruit Gelée with Lemon Mousse and Lime Pound Cake

Chocolate Mousse

Strawberry-Pistachio Trifle

Waffles with Strawberries and Whipped Cream

Strawberries and Cream Tartlets

Cream Cheese Ice Cream with Berry Compote

Pear Medley with a Milkshake Chaser

Apple Tatin with Caramelized Cider Sauce

Caramelized Orange Tartlets

Lemon Tartlets

Vanilla-Poached Rhubarb with Nectarine Compote

Chocolate-Nut Tartlets with Caramel Sauce

Crêpes Suzette

Chocolate Fondant Cake with Earl Grey Tea Sauce

[Bananas Rôties à la Glace Vanille]

Butter-Rum Bananas with Chocolate Sauce and Vanilla Ice Cream *Serves* 6

With bananas, ice cream, chocolate sauce, and whipped cream, this irresistible dessert has all the components of an American banana split. The recipe below adds a fine French touch—a thin, crisp banana tile cookie. (Note that the cookie batter must chill for at least four hours before baking). You can simplify this dessert dramatically by substituting bakery cookies for the tile cookies, store-bought fudge sauce for the chocolate sauce, and canned whipped cream for the homemade variety.

For the banana tile cookies

1 small ripe banana, mashed with a fork
1 large egg white, beaten until frothy
1/3 cup sugar
1/2 cup all-purpose flour, sifted
1/ teaspoon baking powder
3 tablespoons unsalted butter, melted
1/2 cup whole almonds, roasted, cooled, and finely ground in a food processor

For the sautéed bananas

12 tablespoons (1 1/2 sticks) unsalted butter
3/4 cup sugar
9 small ripe bananas, peeled and cut in half lengthwise
1/4 cup dark rum

For the chocolate sauce

7 ounces fine-quality bittersweet chocolate such as Valrhona, chopped into bits
1/2 cup heavy cream
1/4 cup whole milk
1/4 cup sugar

For the garnish

1 quart rich vanilla ice cream (or substitute rum-raisin ice cream)
1 cup Sweetened Whipped Cream (see page 192)

To make the banana tile cookies

In a medium bowl, mash the banana with a fork and set aside. In the bowl of an electric mixer, combine the egg white and the sugar and mix on low until the mixture is frothy and the sugar has dissolved. With the mixer still running, beat in the banana; then add the flour, butter, and ground almonds and mix until smooth. Transfer the mixture to a bowl, cover, and refrigerate for at least 4 hours, or overnight.

Preheat the oven to 375°F. Drop the cookies by the heaping tablespoonful onto a baking sheet covered with parchment paper or a silicone mat, spacing them 3 inches apart. Bake for 22 to 24 minutes, until the cookies turn light golden brown and the edges deep brown. Transfer the baking sheet to a wire rack and cool the cookies for 2 minutes. Then, using a thin metal spatula, lift the cookies gently off the parchment paper and place directly on the rack to cool completely.

To prepare the sautéed bananas

Melt the butter in a large skillet over medium heat. Add the sugar and stir to dissolve. Add half the cut banana and sauté, basting the bananas with the butter, until browned, 5 to 7 minutes. Transfer the sautéed bananas to a plate, and repeat with the remaining half of the bananas, transferring them to the plate when cooked. Add the rum to the skillet, turn off the heat, and swirl the pan to blend. Pour the sauce over the sautéed bananas and keep warm in a low oven.

To prepare the chocolate sauce

Place the chocolate in a medium heatproof bowl and set aside. Combine the cream, milk, and sugar in a medium saucepan, bring to a boil over medium heat, then immediately remove the pan from the heat. Pour the cream mixture over the chocolate and let sit for 30 seconds to allow the chocolate to melt. Whisk the mixture until smooth and set aside.

To serve

Arrange 3 sautéed banana halves in a fan shape on each of six serving plates. Drizzle the butter-rum pan sauce over the bananas, then spoon on the chocolate sauce. Garnish each serving with a scoop of vanilla ice cream, a dollop of sweetened whipped cream, and a banana tile cookie. Serve immediately.

[Vacherin aux Cerises]

Cherry Vacherin

Serves **6**

For the cherry sorbet

1/2 cup sugar

1 pound fresh or individually
   quick-frozen pitted sour cherries

For the vacherins

1/2 pound fresh or individually
   quick-frozen pitted sour cherries,
   plus 6 cherries for garnish

1/2 cup sugar

1 quart rich vanilla ice cream

1 recipe Cherry Sorbet (right),
   or substitute store-bought
   raspberry sorbet

6 pastry rings, 3 inches wide
   by 2 inches high

6 large Vanilla Meringue Cookies
   (see page 193), or substitute
   12 store-bought vanilla meringue
   cookies, crumbled

This beautifully hued dessert is a variation on a classic vacherin, a meringue cake filled with ice cream and fruit, and often topped with whipped cream. To simplify this recipe, you can substitute widely available raspberry sorbet for the homemade cherry sorbet. (If you are going to prepare your own sorbet, begin at least five hours before serving.) To form the vacherins, you will need six 3-inch-wide by 2-inch-high pastry rings; you could also make the dessert in clear glass dessert bowls, but the presentation would not be quite the same. If you wish, serve the vacherin with Sweetened Whipped Cream.

To prepare the cherry sorbet

Combine 2/3 cup of water and the sugar in a saucepan over low heat, stirring to dissolve the sugar. Remove the spoon and let the mixture come to a low simmer without stirring. Cover and simmer, not stirring (stirring can cause the mixture to crystallize), for 2 minutes. Remove from the heat, uncover, and cool to lukewarm before using.

Combine the sugar mixture and the cherries in the bowl of a food processor and purée until smooth. Refrigerate the mixture for 1 to 3 hours to chill. Pour the mixture into the canister of an ice cream maker, and freeze according to the manufacturer's instructions. Store in the freezer at least 2 hours before serving.

To prepare the vacherins

Combine the cherries and sugar in a medium skillet over medium-high heat. Bring to a simmer and cook uncovered for 7 minutes, stirring occasionally, until the cherries are soft. Strain the cherries into a bowl; reserve both the cherries and the sauce.

Spread half of the vanilla ice cream over the bottom of a medium mixing bowl. Cover with a layer of half the cherry sorbet. Repeat the layers with the remaining ice cream and sorbet. Place in the freezer. Remove from the freezer 15 minutes before serving.

Place a pastry ring in the center of each serving plate. Fill the bottom of the rings with the crumbled meringue cookies. Divide the cherry compote among the 6 rings, spooning the mixture over the meringues. Top with a layer of the vanilla ice cream–cherry sorbet mixture, pressing it gently into the molds with the back of a wooden spoon to fill, then smooth the surface with a spatula. Make sure that each spoonful you press into the molds includes both ice cream and sorbet; the mixture should have a swirled look. Spoon the reserved cherry sauce around the vacherins, top each with a whole cherry, and serve immediately, accompanied, if you wish, by Sweetened Whipped Cream (see page 192).

Desserts

For the sauternes gelée

1 envelope (2 1/4 teaspoons)
  unflavored gelatin
1/4 cup sugar
1/2 teaspoon orange zest
2 cups sauternes or muscat wine
4 cups fresh mixed fruits (apple,
  pear, banana, and mango are nice,
  about 1 each; or use 2 fruits,
  2 of each), peeled, seeded and
  cubed; do not use pineapple,
  papaya, or kiwi since these contain
  an enzyme that inhibits the gelatin
  from setting

For the lime mousse

1/2 envelope (1 rounded teaspoon)
  unflavored gelatin
3/4 cup water
1 cup sugar
1/2 cup lime juice (or use lemon
  juice)
1/2 cup Sweetened Whipped Cream
  (see page 192)

For the lime pound cake

Butter and flour for the pan
1 cup self-rising flour, or 1 cup
  all-purpose flour plus 1 teaspoon
  baking powder
3 large eggs
3/4 cup sugar
1/3 cup heavy cream
4 tablespoons unsalted butter,
  softened
Zest of 2 limes (or substitute zest
  of 2 lemons, or 1 orange)

[Gelée de Fruits aux Sauternes]

Sauternes Fruit Gelée with Lemon Mousse and Lime Pound Cake

Serves **6**

To prepare the jelly

Place the gelatin in a medium bowl and set aside. Combine the sugar, orange zest, and sauternes in a small saucepan and bring to a simmer over medium heat, stirring occasionally. Remove from the heat and pour over the gelatin. Stir to dissolve, then set aside to cool. Combine the mixed fruits in a medium bowl, and mix gently. Divide among six Old-Fashioned cocktail glasses or small clear glass bowls. Pour the cooled jelly on top of the fruits and refrigerate for at least 4 hours.

To prepare the lime mousse

Place the gelatin in a medium bowl and set aside. In a small saucepan, combine 3/4 cup water and the sugar and bring to a boil, stirring to dissolve the sugar. Let cool slightly, then pour over the gelatin, stirring to dissolve. Set aside until the mixture is cool to the touch, but not yet set. Add the lime juice and sweetened whipped cream and gently fold in with a spatula or a wooden spoon to incorporate, maintaining as much of the whipped cream's volume as possible. Fill six small ramekins with the mousse and refrigerate 4 to 5 hours.

To prepare the cake

Preheat the oven to 350°F. Butter and flour an 8 1/2 by 4 1/2-inch loaf pan and set aside. Sift the 1 cup self-rising flour into the bowl of an electric mixer, add the eggs, sugar, cream, softened butter, and lime zest and beat on medium just until the batter is smooth. Do not overmix. Scrape the batter into the prepared loaf pan and bake in the center of the oven for 40 to 45 minutes, until golden brown and a toothpick or skewer inserted into the center comes out clean. Transfer the cake to a wire rack to cool in the pan for 15 minutes; then loosen the edges, invert the cake to remove the pan, and place on the cake on the rack to cool completely. Just before serving, cut the cake into 1/4-inch slices.

To serve

Arrange the fruit gelée, mousse, and slices of pound cake on each of six large decorative plates, and serve.

Desserts

[Mousse au Chocolat]

Chocolate Mousse

Serves **6**

For the chocolate mousse

8 ounces high-quality semisweet
  chocolate, such as Valrhona,
  broken into small pieces
5 tablespoons water
2 tablespoons unsalted butter,
  at room temperature
1 tablespoon crème fraîche,
  or heavy cream, at room
  temperature
5 large eggs, separated
  (ideally at room temperature)
Pinch of fine sea salt
2 tablespoons superfine
  or granulated sugar

For the garnish

One 3 1/2-ounce high-quality
  bittersweet chocolate bar,
  such as Valrhona, shaved into curls
  with vegetable peeler

A true French chocolate mousse calls for raw eggs, and this recipe is no exception. (Caveat: There is an occasional risk of salmonella in using raw eggs; if this is a concern, it is best to choose another recipe.) The mousse is delicious alone, garnished simply with shavings of bittersweet chocolate, or, as pictured at right, crowned for a special occasion with a chocolate cup holding a little pool of rich chocolate sauce. You can order chocolate cups that can be used for this purpose from suppliers online; for example, www.lacuisineus.com offers both scalloped chocolate dessert cups and chocolate petit four cups from Switzerland. Or you can make your own from the recipe on page 160, an undertaking that requires patience and precision. It is important to use high-quality imported chocolate in the mousse (never baking chips!) since it makes all the difference in taste and texture. The mousse will be best after chilling at least eight hours or overnight so that the texture firms.

To prepare the mousse

Combine the chocolate with 5 tablespoons of water in the top of a double boiler over gently simmering water, stirring until smooth and shiny. The mixture should never get very hot, just warm to the touch. Remove from the heat. Add the butter and crème fraîche a little at a time and slowly stir in until smooth. Gently and slowly whisk in 1 egg yolk at a time. (Whisking too vigorously, or using eggs that are too cold, can stiffen the chocolate.) Transfer the chocolate mixture to a medium bowl.

Combine the egg whites with the salt in the bowl of an electric mixer and beat until soft peaks form. Add the sugar and beat until stiff but not dry. Add about 1/2 cup of the beaten egg whites to the chocolate mixture and stir gently to combine. Fold in the remaining whites until blended, taking care to maintain as much of the egg whites' volume as possible. Scrape the mousse into a clean bowl, cover loosely, and refrigerate 8 to 24 hours (the longer the better).

To serve

Option #1: Divide the mousse evenly among six glass dessert dishes. Scatter chocolate shavings over the top and serve.

Option #2: Place a chocolate cup on top of each serving of mousse, fill with 2 or 3 tablespoons of the chocolate sauce, and serve.

Desserts

Chocolate Cups

Makes 8 to 10 chocolate cups (allowing for some breakage)

For the chocolate cups

One 7-ounce bar high-quality
bittersweet chocolate, such as
Valrhona, broken into pieces;
reserve 2 tablespoons

Styrofoam egg carton, well-washed,
cut into individual egg cups,
leaving the rims to hold while
working with the chocolate

Note: Preparation of the chocolate cups is a delicate and somewhat tricky operation since chocolate can be a difficult element to work with. You must use a high-quality chocolate with at least 35% cocoa butter content (always noted on the label of a good chocolate), such as Valrhona. And the chocolate has to be at precisely the right temperature at two different moments: It must be heated over a double boiler at a temperature high enough to melt it (115°F), then cooled to 90°F, and worked with rapidly at that point before it gets any cooler. One of the simplest ways to mold the cups is using the individual pockets of a well-washed Styrofoam egg carton.

Melt all but 2 tablespoons of the chocolate in the top of a double boiler over gently simmering water. Bring the chocolate to 115°F on a candy thermometer. Remove from the heat, add the reserved 2 tablespoons of the chocolate, and stir gently to blend. Watch the temperature carefully as the chocolate cools. When the chocolate reaches 90°F it is ideal to work with. (You can actually begin working at a slightly higher temperature, maximum 98°F.) If you don't have a candy thermometer, the chocolate is ready when it feels barely warm to the touch—just about body temperature. Using a pastry brush, apply a thick layer of chocolate to the exterior of the Styrofoam egg cups, painting the chocolate up to the rim; turn upside down and place on a platter or baking sheet to cool for several minutes. As soon as you've finished applying the first coat of the chocolate, apply a thick second coat of chocolate to each cup. If any chocolate remains, and the chocolate is still pliable (you can always rewarm it and cool it down again), paint on a third layer. Chill the cups in the refrigerator for about 3 hours, then slowly and carefully peel away the Styrofoam from the chocolate. The chocolate cups are very fragile, so handle them with care. Store the chocolate cups at room temperature until ready to use.

Chocolate Sauce

Makes 1 cup

Combine the milk, cream, and sugar in a medium saucepan and bring to a boil over medium heat. Remove from the heat, and let cool for 1 minute. Place the chocolate in a medium bowl, then pour the warm milk mixture over the chocolate. Whisk gently until the sauce is blended and glossy. Keep the sauce warm over very low heat until ready to use.

For the chocolate sauce
1/2 cup whole milk
1/4 cup heavy cream
2 tablespoons sugar
4 ounces high-quality bittersweet chocolate, such as Valrhona, broken into bits
1 teaspoon unsweetened cocoa powder

[Notre Fraisier]

Strawberry-Pistachio Trifle

Serves **6**

For the ladyfinger biscuit

3/4 cup granulated sugar

3 large egg yolks

1/2 cup all-purpose flour

1/2 cup cornstarch

5 large egg whites

1 teaspoon confectioners' sugar

For the filling

1/2 cup strawberry syrup (often available in the ice cream section of the market)

2 cups Pastry Cream (see page 192)

1 quart store-bought pistachio ice cream

1/2 pound strawberries, stems removed, cut in half lengthwise

6 whole strawberries with stems

18 raspberries

This colorful layered dessert actually falls somewhere between a trifle and a parfait in style. There are ladyfinger cookies, called biscuit in French, on the bottom, then pastry cream, more cookies, ice cream, and fruit. To simplify this recipe, substitute store-bought ladyfingers (use two for each cookie layer, broken in pieces to fit the glass) instead of the homemade ladyfinger biscuit. You will need six low "whisky on the rocks" type glasses, such as an Old-Fashioned glass, about three inches in diameter. Serve, if you wish, with Strawberry Sauce (page 166).

To prepare the ladyfinger biscuit

Line a large 17 by 11-inch baking sheet with parchment paper and set aside. Preheat the oven to 400°F. Combine 1/2 cup of the granulated sugar with the egg yolks in a large bowl, and whisk until pale yellow. Sift in the flour and cornstarch, and whisk to combine. In a separate bowl, beat the egg whites until soft peaks form; add the remaining 1/4 cup of sugar and beat until stiff peaks form. Fold the whites into the yolk mixture, working gently to maintain as much volume as possible, then spread the mixture into a rectangle about 1/2 inch thick across the prepared baking sheet. Sprinkle with the confectioners' sugar and bake in the center of the oven until lightly golden, 15 to 20 minutes. Transfer the baking sheet to a wire rack to cool.

To assemble and serve

Combine 1/4 cup of the strawberry syrup with 1/4 cup water in a medium bowl and set aside. Combine the 6 whole strawberries, 18 raspberries, and the remaining 1/4 cup strawberry syrup in a medium bowl and set aside. Using the top of one of the serving glasses, cut 12 rounds from the ladyfinger biscuit sheet. (The circles don't have to be perfect, since they are covered by other elements; you can even assemble a cookie layer from broken bits.) Using a pastry brush, coat the cookie rounds with a layer of the strawberry syrup mixture, then place a round in the bottom of each of six serving glasses. Spoon in 1/3 cup of the pastry cream in each glass. Top with another round of biscuit and press in gently. Fill the glasses to the top with pistachio ice cream, smoothing the surface with a small spatula. Slide 7 or 8 strawberry slices into the ice cream around the edges of each glass, cut sides pressing against the glass, the bottoms of the strawberries facing up so that just 1/2 inch or so show above the ice cream. Stir the reserved strawberry-raspberry mixture again, then garnish each serving with a whole strawberry (sliced in half in you wish) and 3 raspberries.

[Gaufres]

Waffles with Strawberries and Whipped Cream

Serves **6**

For the waffle batter

6 tablespoons salted butter
1 1/2 cups whole milk, slightly
  warmed
1 1/4 cup all-purpose flour
1 packet active dry yeast
1/4 cup granulated sugar
4 large eggs, separated

For the garnish

30 strawberries
1/2 cup granulated sugar
Confectioners' sugar
1 cup Sweetened Whipped Cream
  (see page 192)
1 quart rich vanilla ice cream,
  optional

While you can certainly serve these crisp, light waffles for breakfast (without the ice cream!), they are traditionally served in France as a dessert or as a tea-time treat. They are ready in twenty minutes, start to finish. The slightly warmed milk, heated until it is just warm to the touch, helps to keep the batter lump-free.

To prepare the waffles

Preheat the waffle iron. In a small saucepan, melt the butter, add the milk, stir to combine, then heat to just warm. In a medium bowl, combine the flour, yeast, sugar, and egg yolks and whisk to blend. Slowly add the milk mixture and whisk until smooth. In the bowl of an electric mixer, beat the egg whites until stiff. Working with a rubber spatula, carefully fold the egg whites into the batter. Once the egg whites have been incorporated, the waffles must be cooked immediately.

Spoon the batter onto the waffle iron (precisely the amount suggested by the manufacturer). Cook until golden brown, 3 to 5 minutes. Roll the strawberries in the granulated sugar and arrange them on the side of the serving plates. Place the waffles on serving plates and sprinkle with confectioners' sugar. Serve immediately with the Sweetened Whipped Cream and, if you wish, a scoop of vanilla ice cream.

[Tartelettes au Fromage et aux Fraises]

Strawberries and Cream Tartlets

Serves **6**

For the filling
8 ounces fromage blanc,
  or cream cheese, softened
1 large egg
1 egg yolk
Zest of 1 lemon
1/4 cup plus 2 tablespoons sugar
1/2 pound (1 pint) small to medium
  ripe strawberries, trimmed and
  halved

For the tartlets
1 recipe Rich Sugar Pastry Dough
  (see page 191)
  or one 15-ounce package ready-
  made pie crusts, such as Pillsbury
  Rolled Refrigerated Pie Crusts

For the sauce
1 pound strawberries, washed and
  trimmed
1/2 cup sugar

This is a delightful tart for strawberry season, when the berries are sweet, juicy, and red all the way through. The cream filling calls for fromage blanc, a silky, unctuous dairy product with a tangy flavor and the consistency of sour cream. Substituting cream cheese or mascarpone for the fromage blanc changes the consistency and flavor of the tart a bit, but any of the three options makes a fine filling.

To prepare the filling
In a medium bowl, combine the cream cheese, egg, egg yolk, lemon zest, and 1/4 cup sugar and whisk to blend. Set aside until ready to use.

To prepare the tartlets
Preheat the oven to 350°F. On a floured work surface, using a floured rolling pin, roll out the dough to a 1/8-inch-thick rectangle (or, if using 2 round store-bought crusts, roll out to two 1/8-inch-thick circles). Using a 5-inch biscuit cutter or an inverted 5-inch bowl as a guide, cut six 5-inch circles from the dough or store-bought pie crusts. Press the dough gently into the bottoms and sides of six buttered, 4-inch, removable-bottom tart molds, then prick the bottoms of the crusts several times with the tines of a fork. Place the shells on a baking sheet and bake in the center of the oven until golden brown, 10 to 12 minutes. Remove the baking pan from the oven, and reduce the oven temperature to 300°F.

Fill the tartlet shells two-thirds full with the cream cheese mixture, then return to the oven and bake for 5 minutes. Transfer the baking sheet with the tartlets to a wire rack to cool completely. Do not remove the molds until the shells are cooled.

To prepare the strawberry sauce
In a medium saucepan, combine the strawberries and sugar and bring to a simmer over low heat. Simmer for 15 minutes, uncovered, stirring occasionally. Strain the sauce into a bowl through a fine-mesh strainer, cover the bowl, and refrigerate until ready to serve. (Reserve the strained berries for another use, such as a topping for ice cream or sorbet.)

To serve
Working from the outside edge in to the center, arrange the strawberries on top of the cream filling, placing them vertically so that they stand straight up. Sprinkle the tartlets with the remaining 2 tablespoons of sugar. Place a tartlet in the middle of each serving plate, drizzle with the strawberry sauce, and serve.

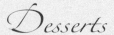

[Coupe Cheesecake]

Cream Cheese Ice Cream with Berry Compote *Serves* 6

For the ice cream

3 large egg yolks
1 cup granulated sugar
2 cups whole milk
3/4 cup heavy cream
4 ounces cream cheese, softened

For the crumble

8 tablespoons (1 stick) unsalted
  butter, well chilled, cut into bits
3/4 cup confectioners' sugar
3/4 cup all-purpose flour
3/4 cup sliced almonds

For the berry compote

1 package unflavored gelatin powder
1 cup raspberries
1 cup strawberries, trimmed
1 cup blackberries
1/4 cup granulated sugar

For the cream sauce

2 cups heavy cream
1/2 cup granulated sugar
1 teaspoon vanilla extract

You prepare four separate elements—ice cream, crumble topping, berry compote, and a vanilla cream sauce—for this striking special-occasion dessert. The ice cream has a lovely, gentle tang from the cream cheese. To save time, you can substitute rich vanilla ice cream for the homemade cream cheese ice cream.

To prepare the ice cream

In a large bowl, whisk together the egg yolks and the sugar until pale and fluffy. Set aside. In a medium saucepan set over medium-high heat, bring the milk and cream to a light boil. In a slow, steady stream, pour the milk mixture into the egg mixture, whisking continuously until smoothly blended. Return the mixture to the saucepan and set over low heat. Stir the mixture constantly with a wooden spoon in a figure-eight motion, until the bubbles on the top of the liquid disappear and the mixture thickens slightly, about 5 minutes. Do not let the mixture boil.

Place the cream cheese in a large bowl, then pour in the hot milk mixture. Whisk vigorously until well blended, then set aside to cool to lukewarm. Process the mixture according to manufacturer's instructions in an ice cream machine to freeze, then place in the freezer for at least 2 hours, or until ready to use.

To prepare the crumble

Preheat the oven to 350°F. Combine the butter, sugar, flour, and almonds into the bowl of a food processor and process until the mixture resembles coarse cornmeal, about 12 seconds. Spread the mixture evenly onto a baking sheet lined with parchment paper or a silicone mat. Bake for 15 to 20 minutes, or until the mixture is golden brown. Remove from the oven and transfer to a wire rack to cool completely.

To prepare the compote

Place the gelatin in a medium bowl and set aside. Combine the raspberries, strawberries, blackberries, and sugar in a medium saucepan. Cook over medium-high heat, stirring frequently but gently with a wooden spoon or spatula, until the berries begin to release their juices, about 5 minutes. Strain the berries in a fine-mesh strainer set over the bowl containing the gelatin so that the warm juice mixes with the gelatin powder; do not press the berries into the strainer. Whisk the mixture well, until all the powder has dissolved. Return the berries to the gelatin mixture, stir gently to combine, and place the bowl in the refrigerator to cool.

To prepare the vanilla sauce

Combine the cream, sugar, and vanilla in a medium saucepan and stir to blend. Bring the mixture to a simmer over medium heat, then reduce the heat to medium-low and simmer, stirring frequently, until the mixture has thickened into a sauce, about 10 minutes. Set aside to cool.

To serve

Divide the fruit compote among six stemmed glass dishes or martini glasses. Place 2 scoops of ice cream in each dish, drizzle with the vanilla sauce, sprinkle with the crumble, and serve immediately.

[Gateau de Poires aux Trois Façons]

Pear Medley with a Milkshake Chaser *Serves* **6**

For the clafoutis

8 tablespoons (1 stick) unsalted
  butter, melted
3/4 cup confectioners' sugar
3/4 cup all-purpose flour
1 tablespoon cornstarch
3/4 cup Pastry Cream
  (see page 192)
2 pears, peeled, cored, and diced,
  or use canned pears and reserve
  the syrup for the granite, below

For the granité

1 1/2 cup granulated sugar
3 cups pear liqueur, or pear syrup
  from canned pears

For the pear compote

1/2 cup granulated sugar
Juice of 1/2 lemon
8 tablespoons (1 stick) unsalted
  butter, cut into bits
3 pears, peeled, halved, and cored

For the milkshake

2 cups vanilla ice cream
1 cup whole milk
5 ice cubes, crushed

Here is a show-stopper dessert, the memorable finale to an elegant dinner. The medley is composed of 3 small, separate pear desserts—a clafoutis, a granité, and a compote— complemented by a fourth element, a vanilla milkshake. Everything but the milkshake can be prepared several hours ahead. You could substitute a cup of canned pears for the fresh in the clafoutis, and then use the pear syrup from the canned pears in the granité instead of the pear liqueur, which makes a rather heady, adults-only dessert!

To prepare the clafoutis

Preheat the oven to 350°F. Combine the melted butter, confectioners' sugar, flour, and cornstarch in a medium bowl. Add the pastry cream, and stir to incorporate. Add the pears and stir gently to combine. Butter six 3- to 4-inch ramekins and fill almost to the brim with the batter. Place the ramekins on a baking sheet and bake in the center of the oven for 30 to 35 minutes, until the edges turn golden brown. Transfer the clafoutis to a wire rack to cool.

To prepare the granité

In a medium saucepan, combine 1 cup of water and the sugar and bring to a boil over high heat, stirring to dissolve the sugar. Remove from the heat and set aside to cool without stirring. Add the pear liqueur, stir to blend, then pour the mixture into a flat baking dish that will fit into your freezer. Place in the freezer and stir with a fork every 30 minutes, to break up the crystals, until frozen and similar in texture to shaved ice; something like a snow cone. Stir every 30 minutes until ready to serve. Spoon into small ramekins.

To prepare the pear compote

Combine the granulated sugar and 1/4 cup of water in a medium saucepan. Place over high heat and bring to a boil, stirring to dissolve the sugar. As soon as the mixture boils, reduce the heat to medium, and cook without stirring until the mixture turns a medium caramel color, 5 to 7 minutes. Remove from the heat, immediately add the lemon juice and butter, and swirl the pan to combine; do not stir. Place the pear halves cut side down in a large skillet, and pour the caramel over the top. Place over low heat and simmer, covered, basting frequently, until the pears are soft, about 15 minutes. Set aside to cool. Thinly slice the cooled pears and divide among six small glass dessert dishes or ramekins.

To prepare the milkshake

Just before serving, combine the vanilla ice cream, milk, and crushed ice in a blender or food processor, and blend until thick and foamy. Pour into six short sherry or juice glasses and serve immediately.

To serve

Arrange the clafoutis, granité, compote, and milkshake on six large, pretty plates—or line them up on individual cutting boards—and serve.

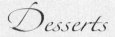

Apple Tatin with Caramelized Cider Sauce

Serves **6**

This apple tatin is a sophisticated version of the classic French tarte tatin, an upside-down apple tart. For the elegant presentation pictured here, you will need six 4-inch cookie or biscuit cutters, or 4-inch pastry rings, to form the individual tarts. You can simplify the presentation by preparing the crusts, apple mixture, and sauce as written, then serving the ensemble more rustically, spooning the apple mixture onto the baked pastry crusts, and topping with a scoop of ice cream. This recipe also works nicely with Bartlett or Comice pears replacing the apples.

For the apple tatin

8 tablespoons (1 stick) unsalted
   butter, cubed, plus more for
   the dish
6 medium Golden Delicious or
   Reinette apples, peeled, cored, and
   quartered, peels and cores reserved
1 cup granulated sugar
2 tablespoons water
Juice of 1/2 lemon

For the sauce

4 tablespoons (1/2 stick) unsalted
   butter
1 1/2 tablespoon light brown sugar
Reserved peels and cores from
   the quartered apples
1 cup apple cider

For the pastry crust

1 recipe Rich Sugar Pastry Dough
   (see page 191) or one 17-ounce
   package ready-made pie-crust
   pastry, such as Pillsbury Rolled
   Refrigerated Pie Crusts

1 pint vanilla ice cream

To prepare the apple tatin

Preheat the oven to 350°F. Place the apples in a buttered 11 by 9-inch baking dish and set aside. In a small saucepan, mix the sugar and water until the sugar dissolves. Place the saucepan over medium-high heat and allow the mixture to boil—without stirring!—until it reaches a light caramel color, 7 to 10 minutes. (Stirring will cause the caramel to crystallize.) When the mixture reaches a caramel color, immediately remove it from the heat and add the lemon juice and butter. Swirl the pan to blend. Pour the caramel over the apples, and place the pan in the center of the oven. Bake until the apples are tender and soft, 35 to 40 minutes.

To prepare the sauce

In a medium saucepan, melt the butter over medium heat. Add the brown sugar and stir to combine. Add the reserved apple peels and cores and stir to combine. Cook, stirring occasionally, for 5 minutes. Add the cider and cook for about 15 minutes, until the mixture thickens and reduces by half. Strain the sauce through a fine-mesh strainer into a bowl and set aside.

To prepare the crust

Preheat the oven to 350°F. On a floured work surface, using a floured rolling pin, roll out the dough into a 1/8-inch-thick rectangle. Cut out six 4-inch circles with a biscuit cutter, or using an inverted 4-inch bowl as a guide. Place the rounds on a baking sheet lined with parchment paper, prick the dough several times with the tines of a fork, then bake in the center of the oven for 10 to 12 minutes, until lightly browned. Transfer the pan to a wire rack to cool.

To assemble the dish

Set a 4-inch biscuit cutter or pastry ring on each of six serving plates. Place a pastry circle in the bottom of each 4-inch biscuit cutter or pastry ring. Divide the apple mixture among the 6 rings, spooning the mixture on top of the pastry crusts. Top each serving with vanilla ice cream, smoothing the surface with a spatula. Carefully remove the biscuit cutters or rings and serve, accompanied by the caramelized cider sauce.

[Tian d'Oranges]

Caramelized Orange Tartlets

Serves **6**

I recipe Rich Sugar Pastry Dough
  (see page 191), or one 15-ounce
  package prepared pie crusts, such
  as Pillsbury Rolled Refrigerated Pie
  Crusts
3/4 cup sugar
2 tablespoons water
12 navel oranges, zest, pith,
  and skin removed, segmented
  and seeded
I cup fresh orange juice
4 tablespoons unsalted butter
3 tablespoons orange marmalade,
  warmed (in the microwave 15 to
  20 seconds) until barely melted
2 cups Sweetened Whipped Cream
  (see page 192)
2 tablespoons apricot jam
12 strips candied orange peel, thinly
  sliced, optional for garnish

These tantalizing sweet-and-sour molded tartlets, filled with caramelized oranges and orange-studded whipped cream, are created in 3-inch-wide by 2-inch-high pastry rings. For a much more rustic, family-style presentation, you can prepare them without the pastry rings: Divide the browned pastry crusts among six serving plates, and spread a teaspoon of marmalade over each. Spoon the caramelized oranges onto the crusts. Top with the orange-flavored whipped cream, garnish as below and serve. Begin preparations several hours ahead of serving, since the components have to chill at several points during the recipe.

Preheat the oven to 350°F. On a floured work surface, using a floured rolling pin, roll out the dough to a 1/8-inch-thick rectangle (or, if using store-bought pastry dough, roll out to two 1/8-inch-thick circles). Using a 3-inch biscuit cutter or an inverted 3-inch bowl as a guide, cut six 3-inch circles from the pastry dough. Prick the bottoms of the crusts several times with the tines of a fork. Place on a baking sheet and bake in the center of the oven for 10 to 12 minutes, until the crusts are golden brown. Remove the baking sheet to a wire rack and let the crusts cool.

Combine the sugar and 2 tablespoons of water in a medium saucepan over high heat. Bring to a boil, stirring to dissolve the sugar, then continue to cook, without stirring, until the mixture turns a light caramel color. Remove from the heat and add the orange juice and butter, and swirl the pan to combine; do not stir. Reduce the heat to low, return the pan to the burner, and cook, stirring frequently, until the mixture begins to thicken, about 5 minutes. Transfer 2 tablespoons of the sauce to a small cup and reserve. Pour the remaining sauce into a heat-proof bowl, add the orange segments, and stir gently with a wooden spoon to combine. Refrigerate for at least I hour.

Drizzle I tablespoon of the warmed marmalade over the sweetened whipped cream and gently fold in. Refrigerate half an hour to I hour. Combine the apricot jam with the reserved 2 tablespoons of the caramel-orange sauce in a small saucepan over low heat, and stir to blend. Set aside.

Spread each pastry crust with I teaspoon of orange marmalade. Place the pastry rings on serving plates and put a crust in the bottom of each ring. Transfer 12 orange segments to a small bowl and reserve; transfer 3 tablespoons of orange sauce to a small cup and reserve. Spoon the remaining oranges equally into each of the rings. Top each serving with 1/3 cup of the sweetened whipped cream mixture, garnish with the reserved orange segments, and drizzle with the apricot jam sauce. Refrigerate for I hour before serving. Spoon the reserved caramel-orange sauce around the plate, garnish with the candied orange peel, if you wish, and serve.

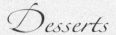

[Mini Tartelettes au Citron]

Lemon Tartlets

Serves **6**

For the pastry crust

1 recipe Rich Sugar Pastry Dough
(see page 191), or one 15-ounce
package prepared pie crusts,
such as Pillsbury Rolled
Refrigerated Pie Crusts

For the lemon filling

3 large egg yolks
3/4 cup confectioners' sugar
1/2 cups fresh lemon juice, strained
6 tablespoons (3/4 stick) unsalted
butter, melted
2 tablespoons superfine sugar
Lemon Confit (see page 187), or zest
of 1 lemon

The tart, tangy lemon curd filling in these tempting tartlets contrasts beautifully with the crunchy sweetness of the rich pastry crust. The tarts need to chill for at least half an hour before serving to properly firm.

To prepare the tartlet shells

Preheat the oven to 350°F. On a floured work surface, using a floured rolling pin, roll out the dough to a 1/8-inch-thick rectangle (or, if using store-bought pastry dough, roll out to two 1/8-inch-thick circles). Using a 5-inch biscuit cutter or an inverted 5-inch bowl as a guide, cut six 5-inch circles from the pastry dough. Press the dough gently into the bottoms and sides of six buttered, 4-inch, removable-bottom tart molds, then prick the bottoms of the crusts several times with the tines of a fork. Line the tartlet shells with aluminum foil or parchment paper, then fill to the brim with baking weights or dried beans. Place on a baking sheet and bake the tartlet shells in the center of the oven for 8 minutes. Remove the baking weights and the foil, return the shells to the oven and bake for 10 to 12 minutes more, until the crusts are golden brown. Remove the baking pan from the oven and transfer the tartlets, still on the baking sheet, to a wire rack. Reduce the oven temperature to 300°F.

To prepare the lemon filling

Combine the egg yolks and sugar in a medium bowl and whisk until the mixture is smooth and pale yellow. Add the lemon juice and then the melted butter, each in a slow steady stream, whisking continuously to incorporate. Ladle the lemon mixture into the cooled tartlet shells, sprinkle the tops with the superfine sugar, and bake for 3 minutes. Turn the oven off, but let the tartlets remain in the oven for another 10 minutes. Remove the tartlets from the oven and transfer, still in their pans, to a wire rack to cool to room temperature, then refrigerate for at least 30 minutes. To serve, remove the tartlets from their pans, garnish with a few strands of Citron Confit or lemon zest, and serve.

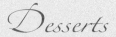

[Rhubarbe Cuite à la Vanille]

Vanilla-Poached Rhubarb with Nectarine Compote

Serves **6**

For the rhubarb

2 cups water
1/2 cup granulated sugar
1 pound rhubarb, peeled and cut into
  4-inch pieces
1/2 teaspoon vanilla extract

For the nectarine compote

4 tablespoons unsalted butter
3/4 cup granulated sugar
5 nectarines or peaches, peeled and
  cut into chunks

For the berry garnish

1 cup fresh whole strawberries,
  or frozen strawberries, thawed
3 tablespoons confectioners' sugar
1 teaspoon fresh lemon juice
2 cups (1 pint) fresh strawberries,
  washed and thinly sliced
1/2 pound fresh raspberries

A lovely, light dessert, this four-fruit combination has a refreshing sweet-and-sour flavor, perfect after a rich meal. Garnish if you wish with a lacy tuile, or tile cookie (page 192), or a light, delicate cookie from your favorite bakery. You can prepare the rhubarb and the nectarine compote several hours, or even a day, ahead.

To prepare the rhubarb

Combine 2 cups of water and the sugar in a medium saucepan, and bring to a boil over medium-high heat. Stir to dissolve the sugar. Add the rhubarb and vanilla, reduce the heat to low and simmer for about 10 minutes, stirring occasionally, or until soft but not limp. Set aside to cool.

To prepare the nectarine compote

Melt the butter in a large skillet over medium-high heat. Add the sugar and nectarines and cook, stirring frequently, until browned and bubbling, about 7 minutes. Reduce the heat to low and simmer, stirring occasionally, for 10 minutes. Set aside to cool, then transfer to a bowl, cover, and refrigerate until ready to use.

To assemble and serve

Combine the whole strawberries, confectioners' sugar, and lemon juice in the bowl of a food processor or blender and purée until smooth. Set aside. Arrange 4 sticks of rhubarb side by side on each of six serving plates. Cover each serving with a layer of the nectarine compote. Top with a row of raspberries down the center and a row of sliced strawberries along each side. Spoon the puréed strawberry sauce over the berries. Garnish with a tile cookie if you wish, and serve.

[Mini Tartelettes Choco-Caramel]

Chocolate-Nut Tartlets with Caramel Sauce

Serves **6**

These luscious, gooey tartlets get their crunch from a beautifully textured mix of walnuts, pistachios, and pine nuts. Try them with a little scoop of rich vanilla ice cream on the side. Note that the dough needs to chill for three hours.

For the pastry dough

1 cup all-purpose flour
3/4 cup unsalted butter
1/4 cup sugar
1 tablespoon unsweetened cocoa powder
1 whole egg

For the filling

1/4 cup plus 2 tablespoons sugar
1/3 cup light cream
1 cup walnuts, coarsely chopped
1/2 cup pine nuts
1 cup pistachios, coarsely chopped

To prepare the pastry dough

In the bowl of a food processor, combine the flour, butter, sugar, and cocoa powder and process until the mixture resembles coarse cornmeal. Add the egg and pulse 12 to 14 times, just until the dough begins to hold together in a mass, but before it becomes a ball. Press the dough into a disk, wrap in plastic wrap, and refrigerate for 3 hours.

Preheat the oven to 350°F. Divide the dough into 6 equal pieces. Working on a lightly floured surface (the dough is sticky), flatten or roll out each portion into a disk roughly 5 inches in diameter; the dough is very malleable. (If you use a rolling pin, coat it with a bit of flour before rolling.) Press the dough into the bottoms and sides of six buttered, 4-inch tartlet molds. Prick the bottoms of the tart shells with a fork. Bake in the center of the oven for 10 minutes, until the dough is lightly browned. Set the tartlets on a wire rack to cool.

To prepare the filling

In a medium skillet, combine the sugar and 2 tablespoons of water over high heat. Do not stir. Bring the mixture to a boil, then cook, still not stirring, until the mixture turns a rich brown caramel color. Remove from the heat immediately, add the cream, and swirl the pan to blend. Add the walnuts, pine nuts, and pistachios and mix well with a wooden spoon to combine.

To serve

Using an ice cream scoop, mound the caramel-nut mixture filling into the tartlet shells. Serve warm.

Desserts

Crêpes Suzette

Serves **6** *to* **7** *(makes 12 to 15 crêpes)*

For the crêpe batter

4 tablespoons salted butter
2 cups whole milk
4 large egg yolks
1 1/2 tablespoon sugar
1 3/4 cups all-purpose flour
1 tablespoon sunflower oil
Zest of 1 orange, finely grated
Zest of 1 lemon, finely grated

For the Suzette butter

1/3 cup sugar
Juice of 4 or 5 medium oranges
1 teaspoon lemon juice
8 tablespoons (1 stick) unsalted
   butter, chilled and cut into bits
1/4 cup Grand Marnier
   (orange liqueur)

For the garnish

4 oranges, peeled, zest, pith,
   skin removed, cut into sections,
   and seeded
2 ounces candied orange peel,
   very thinly sliced, optional

You may have memories of elaborate restaurant meals crowned as a finale by a pan of flaming crêpes Suzette prepared tableside. But flaming crêpes Suzette are just one version of this beloved, classic French dessert. Other versions, such as this delicate, refined recipe, are not flamed with brandy. These crêpes are brightened by lemon and orange zest in the batter. Just before serving they're bathed in a fresh orange juice and Grand Marnier sauce. You'll never miss the flames!

To prepare the batter

Combine the butter and milk in a microwave-safe dish and heat on high power in the microwave for 1 minute, or until the butter is melted. In a medium bowl, combine the egg yolks and sugar, and whisk to blend. Add the flour and whisk to blend. Add the butter mixture a little bit at a time, whisking to blend each time. Add the sunflower oil and the citrus zests and whisk to blend.

Heat a nonstick griddle or a nonstick crêpe pan (or a crêpe pan coated with nonstick cooking spray) over medium-high heat. Pour 1/4 cup of the batter on the griddle or in the pan to form a circle. Cook for approximately 1 minute, or until golden brown. Flip and cook on the opposite side for 45 seconds, until golden brown. Place the crêpes on a platter and keep warm in a low oven until ready to serve.

To prepare the Suzette butter

Combine the sugar, orange, and lemon juice in a medium saucepan and set over medium heat. Bring the mixture to a boil, stirring occasionally, and reduce by half, about 10 minutes. Whisk in the butter a little at a time, until completely incorporated. Stir in the Grand Marnier and keep warm in the pan over very low heat.

To serve

Fold the crêpes in half, and then in half again, placing 2 on each serving plate. Drizzle with the Suzette butter, garnish with orange wedges and, if you wish, a few strips of candied orange peel, and serve immediately. As an alternate way of serving, arrange all of the crêpes on a warmed platter, drizzle with the Suzette butter, garnish decoratively with the orange wedges and, if you wish, a few strips of candied orange peel. Serve family-style at the table.

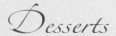

Desserts

Chocolate Fondant Cake with Earl Grey Tea Sauce

Serves **6**

For the chocolate fondant

One 3 1/2-ounce bar high-quality bittersweet dark chocolate, such as Valrhona, broken into bits

One 3 1/2-ounce bar high-quality milk chocolate, such as Valrhona, broken into bits

3 large egg yolks

1/4 cup sugar

1 1/4 cup Sweetened Whipped Cream (see page 192)

For the chocolate streusel

8 tablespoons (1 stick) cold unsalted butter

1/2 cup sugar

1 1/2 cups all-purpose flour

1/4 cup unsweetened cocoa powder

1 teaspoon finely crushed Earl Grey tea leaves

For the caramelized tea sauce

1/2 cup light brown sugar, well packed

1 teaspoon finely crushed Earl Grey tea leaves

For the garnish

One 3 1/2-ounce bar high-quality milk chocolate, such as Valrhona, chilled, shaved into curls with a vegetable peeler

Is it fudge? Is it cake? You decide! It's officially a flourless "soft cake" that is incredibly rich, unctuous, and chocolaty—a confection for chocolate lovers that's sprinkled with a chocolate and Earl Grey tea streusel topping and drizzled with a tea-speckled caramel syrup.

To prepare the fondant

Line an 8-inch square baking pan or dish with parchment paper or plastic wrap, with the ends extending well beyond the edges of the pan. Place the bittersweet and milk chocolate in a double boiler over simmering water, and melt over low heat. Set aside and let cool to lukewarm, 90°F on a candy thermometer. Combine the egg yolks with the sugar in a small bowl, and whisk until pale. Add the melted chocolate and whisk to blend. Add the sweetened whipped cream and gently fold into the chocolate mixture. Scrape into the prepared baking pan and smooth the surface with a small spatula. Place in the freezer for at least 3 hours.

To prepare the streusel

Preheat the oven to 350°F. In the bowl of a food processor, combine the butter, sugar, flour, cocoa powder, and tea leaves and pulse until a coarse mixture the consistency of wet sand forms. Crumble onto a baking sheet lined with parchment paper or a silicone mat, and bake in the center of the oven for 15 minutes, stirring the crumbs with a spatula halfway through. Set aside on a wire rack to cool.

To prepare the streusel

Combine the brown sugar and 1/4 cup of water in a small saucepan over medium heat, and bring to a boil. Remove from the heat and add the tea leaves, gently swirling the pan to combine. Set aside to infuse until the mixture cools.

To serve

One hour before serving, gently lift the fondant from the mold, transfer to a large plate, and set aside at room temperature. When ready to serve, run a cake knife under hot water for several seconds, then slice the fondant into 6 equal slices and place on serving plates. Sprinkle each serving with the chocolate streusel, drizzle the tea sauce around the plate, and decorate with the chocolate shavings and serve.

Basics

The following recipes fall into one of two categories: There are fundamental recipes for components of other dishes featured in these pages, such as pastry crusts, tomato confit, garlic confit, chicken stock, and court bouillon. There are also a handful of very simple, traditional recipes, such as those for tapenade, whipped cream, macaroni gratin, and tile cookies that are fine accompaniments not only to recipes in this book, but to many other dishes, and occasions, as well.

Tomates Confites / *Tomato Confit*

15 medium garden-fresh
 or vine-ripened tomatoes,
 peeled, quartered lengthwise,
 seeds and membranes removed
6 tablespoons extra-virgin olive oil
15 basil sprigs, stems removed,
 leaves sliced in thin strips
1/2 teaspoon sugar
Fine sea salt
Freshly ground black pepper
3 garlic cloves, peeled and crushed

These intensely flavored, slow-baked tomatoes with a satiny texture are often called for in this book. They add rich flavor and color to tarts, salads, gratins, and side dishes. You can store them, covered with extra-virgin olive oil, in a sealed jar for up to three days. For best results, use garden-fresh tomatoes, or tomatoes purchased still attached to the vine.

Preheat the oven to 180ºF, or the lowest setting. In a large mixing bowl, combine all the ingredients except for the garlic and very gently toss them with your hands to just combine. Arrange the tomato mixture on a baking sheet greased with olive oil, scatter on the garlic pieces, and place in the center of the oven. Bake for 2 1/2 to 3 hours, turning them once halfway through the cooking process. The tomatoes will contract and dry a bit during baking as they lose their moisture, but should still be plump when you remove them from the oven. Set aside in the pan to cool, then transfer the tomatoes, along with the garlic, to a plate. Cover the plate with plastic wrap and refrigerate the confit, several hours or overnight, until ready to use.

Confit de Citron / *Citron Confit*

Use these sweet-and-sour lemon strips to garnish lemon tarts, fish, and shellfish. Make Citron Confit at least twenty-four hours ahead of using.

Combine the lemon zest, lemon juice, and sugar in a saucepan and bring to a boil over high heat, stirring to dissolve the sugar. Reduce the heat to medium low and cook, stirring frequently, until the mixture is thick and syrupy, 6 to 10 minutes. Cool, then cover and let stand overnight. Store in a sealed jar in a cool place.

Makes about 1 cup
Zest of 6 lemons, cut into very thin strips
Juice of 5 lemons
6 sugar cubes, or 6 teaspoons sugar

Gousses d'Ail Confites / *Garlic Confit*

These soft, savory garlic cloves, slow-cooked in olive oil, are delicious spread on slices of toasted baguette, or served as a side dish to roast chicken. The olive oil that the garlic cooks in becomes perfumed with garlic and can be used in flavorful salad dressings, or just for dipping into with crusty country bread.

Preheat the oven to 200°F. Combine the garlic cloves, thyme, rosemary, and olive oil in a small casserole, cover, and place in the center of the oven. Bake for 1 1/2 hours. Set aside to cool; discard the rosemary and thyme. Transfer the garlic, oil, and herbs to a glass jar with a strong seal, such as a Ball jar, and refrigerate for up to a month. Bring to room temperature before serving.

30 garlic cloves, unpeeled
1 branch thyme
1 branch rosemary
2 cups extra-virgin olive oil

Beurre d'Escargot / *Garlic-Shallot Butter*

This deliciously savory butter is sometimes known as "snail butter" since it is the traditional butter mixture in which escargots are prepared. It is also an excellent choice for glazing vegetable side dishes, especially the ultrathin green beans known as haricots verts. You can easily double this recipe and freeze it, wrapped well in plastic wrap.

Combine the butter, prosciutto, garlic, shallot, parsley, and a pinch of salt and pepper, and mix well. Transfer the butter to a ramekin, or form into a log by rolling and sealing in plastic wrap; refrigerate or freeze.

8 tablespoons (1 stick) unsalted butter, softened
1 slice (about 1 ounce) prosciutto or other cured ham, minced
1/2 garlic clove, finely chopped
1/2 medium shallot, finely chopped
1/4 cup finely chopped flat-leaf parsley
Fine sea salt
Freshly ground black pepper

Beurre Clarifié / *Clarified Butter*

8 tablespoons (1 stick) unsalted
butter, cut into bits

Clarified butter (also called "drawn butter") removes the impurities—the milk solids—and the water from the butter, leaving a pure, clear, golden butterfat. The resulting butter, clarified of its impurities, has a much higher smoke point than regular butter, which means that it can cook longer at higher heat than unclarified butter. Chefs use it often in sauces and sautéed dishes. With the milk solids removed, this butter turns rancid much less quickly than regular butter. You can make a large batch of clarified butter and store it in the refrigerator, sealed, for a couple of months.

Microwave: Place the butter in a 1- or 2-cup microwave-safe measuring cup or large ramekin. Microwave the butter on high for 1 1/2 minutes. Remove and set aside for 1 minute. Skim off the foamy top layer, then spoon the clear butter into small bowl; this is the clarified butter. Discard the milky residue at the bottom of the measuring cup. Use immediately, or cover, cool, and refrigerate for up to 2 months.

If you prefer to clarify the butter on the stovetop: Place the butter in a heavy-bottom saucepan over low heat. Simmer the butter very slowly, skimming off any white foam that rises to the top; skim frequently. After 12 to 15 minutes, the solids in the butter will sink to the bottom of the pan. Remove the pan from the heat and set aside for 4 minutes. Spoon the clarified butter into a small bowl or clean jar. The clarified butter will keep, well covered in the refrigerator, for up to 2 months.

Court Bouillon

1 medium onion, chopped
1 small carrot, chopped
1/2 celery stalk, chopped
1 1/2 cups dry white wine
4 cups cold water
1 thyme sprig
3 flat-leaf parsley sprigs
2 bay leaves
1 teaspoon whole black peppercorns
1 teaspoon fine sea salt
1/2 cup white wine vinegar

Court bouillon ("quick broth") is a clear, vegetable-based stock that is used for poaching fish and shellfish, as well as the basis for many sauces and soups. There are many variations on this classic, some even including lemon balm, ginger, and Szechuan peppers. You can add a clove of garlic, a pinch of ground cloves, or 1/2 teaspoon of coriander seeds, or substitute red wine for white, or red wine vinegar for white wine vinegar. It's a versatile and adaptable recipe. The recipe below is for a light, aromatic, traditional court bouillon.

Combine all the ingredients except the vinegar in a large saucepan and bring to a boil over high heat. Reduce the heat to medium-low and cook for 5 minutes. Add the vinegar and cook for 15 minutes. Remove from the heat, set aside to cool, then pour through a fine-mesh strainer into a large bowl. You can keep court bouillon, covered, in the refrigerator for 3 days, or freeze in an airtight container for 1 month.

Fond Blanc de Volaille / *Chicken Stock*

In a large stockpot, combine the chicken with enough cold water to cover. Bring to a boil over high heat, then boil for 5 minutes, skimming the surface frequently. Transfer the chicken to a colander placed in the sink, and rinse well under cold running water to remove any traces of scum. Discard the cooking water and clean the pot to remove the scum. Return the chicken to the pot and cover with cold water. Add the onions, leek, carrots, celery stalks, tomato, parsley, salt, and peppercorns and bring to a boil over high heat. Reduce the heat and cook, uncovered, at a low simmer for 2 hours, without stirring or skimming. Remove from the heat and set aside to cool. Strain the stock through a fine-mesh strainer or a colander lined with three layers of cheesecloth into a large bowl. Let the stock cool completely, then store, covered, in the refrigerator for up to 24 hours.

6 to 7 pounds raw chicken parts, including wings, backs, and necks
2 medium onions, quartered
1 large leek (green parts only), rinsed well and cut into 2-inch pieces
3 medium carrots, peeled and quartered
2 celery stalks, cut into 2-inch pieces
1 medium tomato, quartered and seeded
6 parsley stems
1 tablespoon coarse sea salt
1 teaspoon whole black peppercorns

Tapenade / *Provençal Olive Paste*

In a blender or mini food processor, combine the olives, capers, lemon juice, garlic, sherry vinegar, a pinch of salt, pepper to taste, and the olive oil. Purée until the mixture forms a thick, smooth paste

1 cup Niçoise or small Kalamata olives, pitted
1 tablespoon capers, drained and coarsely chopped
1/4 teaspoon lemon juice
1/2 garlic clove
1 tablespoon sherry vinegar
Fine sea salt
Freshly ground black pepper
1/4 cup extra-virgin olive oil

Vinaigrette à la Tomate / *Tomato Vinaigrette*

This is an unusual, fresh, and very tasty vinaigrette made with the tomato water drained from tomatoes used in other recipes. It's delicious on a green bean salad, or a Niçoise-style salad.

Combine the "tomato water," sherry wine vinegar, and a pinch of salt and pepper and whisk to dissolve the salt. Add the olive oil and whisk to blend.

3 to 4 tablespoons drained "tomato water"
1 tablespoon sherry wine vinegar
Fine sea salt
Freshly ground black pepper
5 tablespoons extra-virgin olive oil

Caviar d'Aubergines / *Eggplant Caviar*

Eggplant caviar, a popular hors d'oeuvre spread in the south of France, is usually served with slices of toasted baguette, but it's also tasty on celery sticks, bread sticks, or fennel fronds. It also makes a nice side dish, served with baguette toasts, to accompany fish dishes.

To prepare the eggplant caviar: Preheat the oven to 300°F. Slice both ends from the eggplants, make 3 small slits in each, and stuff the garlic cloves into the flesh. Wrap the eggplants individually in aluminum foil and bake for 50 minutes. Let cool slightly in the foil. Cut the eggplants in half lengthwise and scoop out the pulp with a spoon. Heat the olive oil in a large skillet over medium-high heat. Add the eggplant pulp and sauté, stirring frequently, until any excess liquid has evaporated, 8 to 10 minutes. Add the curry powder, lemon juice, and olives, and mix well. Remove from the heat to cool, then transfer the mixture to the bowl of a food processor. Purée for about 10 seconds, until the mixture is smoothly blended. Season to taste with salt and pepper. Serve at room temperature with baguette toasts.

Serves 6

For the eggplant caviar
4 small eggplants (10 to 12 ounces each)
3 garlic cloves, peeled and quartered
4 tablespoons extra-virgin olive oil
1/4 teaspoon curry powder
Juice of 1/2 lemon
1/4 cup pitted black olives
Fine sea salt
Freshly ground black pepper

Purée d'Aubergines / *Eggplant Purée*

4 small eggplants (10 to 12 ounces each)
4 tablespoons extra-virgin olive oil
Fine sea salt
Freshly ground black pepper

Although similar to Eggplant Caviar, this eggplant recipe has its own character, mild and very versatile. This purée makes a nice side dish to a roast rack of pork, or grilled chicken. It has the almost-smooth consistency of mashed potatoes, and would make a great potato substitute for those on a low-carbohydrate diet.

Preheat the oven to 300°F. Slice both ends from the eggplants, then wrap the eggplants individually in aluminum foil and bake for 50 minutes. Let cool slightly in the foil. Cut the eggplants in half lengthwise and scoop out the pulp with a spoon. Heat the olive oil in a large skillet over medium-high heat. Add the eggplant pulp and sauté, stirring frequently, until any excess liquid has evaporated, 8 to 10 minutes. Season to taste with salt and pepper. Transfer to the bowl of a food processor, and pulse 5 or 6 times, until almost smooth. Return to the skillet and keep warm over low heat until ready to serve.

Gratin de Macaroni / *Macaroni Gratin*

Serves 6

8 tablespoons (1 stick) unsalted butter
1 pound elbow pasta
3 cups chicken stock
1 cup heavy cream
1/2 cup mascarpone cheese
Fine sea salt
Freshly ground black pepper
1/2 cup grated Reggiano Parmesan

This mild, creamy, and luscious gratin is a delicious accompaniment to roast chicken or a roast leg of lamb, or the Fricassee of Veal Kidneys on page 104. It's a dish children will love, too, a variation on a classic Mac-Cheese.

Melt the butter in a large saucepan over medium-high heat. Add the pasta and stir to coat. Add the chicken stock, stir to combine, and cook until all the liquid has been completely absorbed, about 8 minutes. Add the cream and mascarpone, stir to combine, and continue to cook for an additional 2 to 3 minutes, stirring occasionally. Season to taste with salt and pepper, then transfer the mixture to a 12-inch oval gratin dish or other medium baking dish. Sprinkle the top with the Reggiano Parmesan, and place under the broiler until the top is golden brown and bubbling, 2 to 3 minutes. Serve hot.

Dentelles de Parmesan / *Lacy Parmesan Crisps*

Makes 10 crisps

1 cup finely grated Reggiano Parmesan cheese, or other fine Parmesan
1 tablespoon all-purpose flour
1 teaspoon unsalted butter

These delicate, lacy cheese crisps, ready in seconds, are a delicious, tangy treat served with apéritifs, or as an accompaniment to dishes such as the Mille-feuilles of Crispy Potatoes, page 128. You can prepare them flat, like a traditional cracker, or place them on a rolling pin or wine bottle to cool into a curved "tuile" shape, like a tile cookie.

Combine the Parmesan and flour together in a medium bowl, rubbing the mixture between your fingertips to blend. Heat a small, 6-inch nonstick skillet over medium heat, then brush a tiny dab of butter across the bottom of the pan. Sprinkle a heaping tablespoon of the mixture into a 5-inch circle, using just enough to cover the surface of the circle. Heat for 12 to 20 seconds, just until the cheese starts to bubble all over. Remove from the heat, tilt the pan and delicately slide a metal spatula under the crisp and transfer it to a fine-mesh wire rack to cool; or transfer it to a rolling pin to form into a curved "tile cookie" shape, wait 10 to 15 seconds for it to set, then place on a wire rack to cool. Repeat with the remaining cheese mixture. Serve immediately.

Pâte à Foncer / *Flaky Short-Crust Dough*

Combine the flour, butter, and salt in a food processor. Process about 12 seconds, until the mixture has a dry, crumbly texture resembling coarse cornmeal. Add the egg and the water and pulse 12 to 14 times, just until the dough begins to hold together in a mass, but before it turns into a ball. (Do not overprocess; the crust can become tough if the dough is processed even a few seconds too long.) If the dough is too dry and dense, add 1 to 2 more tablespoons of water and pulse 2 or 3 more times. Remove the dough from the mixing bowl, work it into a ball in your hands, then flatten it into a disk. Wrap the disk in plastic wrap and refrigerate for at least 1 hour.

Makes enough dough for one 9 1/2- to 11-inch tart, or six 4-inch tartlets

- 1 1/2 cups all-purpose flour
- 8 tablespoons (1 stick) unsalted butter, chilled and cut into small bits
- 1/2 teaspoon salt
- 1 large egg, beaten
- 4 tablespoons ice water

Pâte à Barbajuan / *"Uncle John" Olive Oil Pastry Dough*

Combine the flour, olive oil, and salt in a food processor. Process about 12 seconds, until the mixture has a dry, crumbly texture resembling coarse cornmeal. Add the egg and the water and pulse 12 to 14 times, just until the dough begins to hold together in a mass, but before it turns into a ball. (Do not overprocess; the crust can become tough if the dough is processed even a few seconds too long.) If the dough is too dry and dense, add 1 to 2 more tablespoons of water and pulse 2 or 3 more times. If the dough is too sticky, add 1 to 2 tablespoons of flour and pulse 2 or 3 more times. Remove the dough from the mixing bowl, work it into a ball in your hands, then flatten it into a disk. Wrap the disk in plastic wrap and refrigerate for at least 1 hour.

Makes enough dough for one 11- to 13-inch pastry crust or 18 to 20 Barbajuan purses

- 2 cups all-purpose flour
- 1/4 cup extra-virgin olive oil
- 1 teaspoon fine sea salt
- 1 large egg
- 1/2 cup ice water

Pâte Sablée / *Rich Sugar Pastry Dough*

Combine the butter, confectioners' sugar, egg, vanilla, and salt in a food processor and process about 7 seconds, until blended. Add the flour 1/2 cup at a time, pulsing 2 or 3 times after each addition, until the flour is blended and the dough just comes together; do not let the dough form a ball. The dough should be pliable but not sticky. If the dough is sticky, add 2 more tablespoons of flour and process for a few seconds until blended.

Remove the dough from the bowl, knead it between your hands for about 1 minute, then press it into a flat disk. Wrap the disk in plastic wrap and refrigerate for at least 1 hour, or even overnight.

Makes enough dough for one 9 1/2- to 11-inch tart, or six 4-inch tartlets

- 10 tablespoons (1 1/4 sticks) unsalted butter, cut into bits and slightly softened
- 1/2 cup confectioners' sugar
- 1 large egg, beaten
- 1/2 teaspoon vanilla extract
- 1/2 teaspoon salt
- 1 1/2 cups all-purpose flour

Crème Chantilly / *Sweetened Whipped Cream*

1 cup heavy cream, well chilled
2 tablespoons confectioners' sugar
1/2 teaspoon vanilla extract, or
  1 teaspoon vanilla sugar,
  optional

In the bowl of an electric mixer, combine the cream, sugar, and vanilla extract. Beat on medium speed, scraping down the sides of the bowl occasionally, until soft peaks form. Cover with plastic wrap and refrigerate until ready to use. Whipped cream is always best used within 2 hours of beating.

Crème Pâtissière / *Pastry Cream*

1 1/2 cups whole milk
1/2 vanilla bean, split, or
  1/2 teaspoon vanilla extract
4 large egg yolks
1/4 cup sugar
2 tablespoons cornstarch
1 tablespoon unsalted butter

In a heavy-bottomed saucepan, bring the milk to a boil over medium heat. If you are using a vanilla bean, add it now, cover the pan, remove it from the heat, and set aside for 10 minutes to infuse. Combine the egg yolks and sugar in a glass or ceramic mixing bowl, then whisk briskly for about 2 minutes, until the mixture is thick and pale yellow. Add the cornstarch and whisk to blend. Remove the vanilla bean, if used, from the milk. If a skin has formed over the milk, remove it. Slowly add the milk to the egg mixture, whisking until blended and smooth.

Return the mixture to the saucepan and bring to a boil, whisking constantly over medium heat. Reduce the heat to low and cook at a simmer, whisking constantly so that the bottom won't burn, for about 1 minute, until thick, smooth, and yellow. Remove from the heat, add the butter, and stir to blend. If you are using vanilla extract, stir it in now. Transfer the mixture to a bowl and cover with a sheet of plastic wrap pressed directly on the surface of the pastry cream to prevent a skin from forming. Cool, then refrigerate the cream for at least 1 hour, or even overnight. (Pastry cream can be made up to a day ahead and refrigerated.)

Tuiles aux Amandes / *Almond Tile Cookies*

Makes about twelve 3-inch cookies

2 cups finely sliced blanched
  almonds
1 1/2 cups sugar
6 large egg whites, beaten until
  frothy
6 tablespoons all-purpose flour,
  sifted
1 teaspoon vanilla extract
4 tablespoons (1/2 stick) unsalted
  butter, melted

Combine the almonds and sugar in a large mixing bowl, and stir together with a wooden spoon. Add the egg whites and stir to combine. Sprinkle the flour into the bowl, stirring to combine. Add the vanilla and melted butter and stir until blended. Cover the batter and refrigerate at least 1 hour.

Preheat the oven to 375°F. You may have to bake the cookies in two batches; or bake half now and the other half within 5 days, keeping the batter well sealed in the refrigerator. Butter a large baking sheet, or line with a sheet of parchment paper. Prepare two or three (washed) wine bottles laid on their sides, or a couple of rolling pins, to drape the cookies on. Drop the batter onto the sheet, using 1 heaping tablespoon per cookie. Space them about 3 inches apart. Gently flatten each cookie, making it as round and thin as possible. Bake in the center of the oven until golden brown at the edges and pale in the centers, 7 to 9 minutes. Cool in the pan on a wire rack for about 2 minutes, just until the cookies set but are still warm and flexible. Using a thin metal spatula, gently loosen the cookies from the baking sheet, releasing the edges first and working toward the center, and carefully drape them over the bottles so that they softly curve. If the cookies cool too fast and become stiff, return them on the baking sheet to the still-warm oven for 30 to 45 seconds, then immediately drape them over the bottles. Cool completely before serving.

Meringues / *Vanilla Meringue Cookies*

Meringues can go limp and lose their crunch on a hot, humid day. It's best not to make these cookies in the middle of summer. You can make pastel-hued meringues—pale pink, pale green, pale yellow—by adding a drop or two of food coloring to the egg whites when you add the confectioners' sugar.

Preheat the oven to 200°F. Line 2 baking sheets with lightly buttered parchment paper, buttered side up, or line with a silicone baking mat. Beat the egg whites with an electric mixer at medium speed until they begin to form soft peaks. Gradually add the granulated sugar, beating until the whites are stiff but not dry. Add the confectioners' sugar a little at a time and gently fold it in with a rubber spatula. Add the vanilla extract and gently fold in. Using a pastry bag, pipe 12 to 16 meringues into circles about 2 inches wide and 2 inches high onto the baking sheet. Space them about 1 inch apart. (You can also form meringues by hand, using a tablespoon to shape the meringue mixture into 12 to 16 spheres.)

Bake for 1 1/2 to 2 hours, with the handle of a wooden spoon holding the oven door slightly ajar. Watch carefully as the meringues bake; they should barely take on any color, turning pale beige at the most. They should be crisp on the outside but slightly soft within, not dry and crunchy all the way through. If the meringues begin to brown too quickly, lower the oven heat by a notch. Cool on a wire rack, then set aside in a dry place until ready to serve. Meringues are always best within a day of baking.

Makes 12 to 16 meringue cookies

1 cup egg whites (about 8 large)
1 cup granulated sugar
2 cups confectioners' sugar
1 teaspoon vanilla extract

Source Guide

Restaurants

For further information or reservations at any of the restaurants of Alain Ducasse
or at Sophie Dudemaine's Maison de Sophie, please contact them directly.
For any properties outside the United States, you must dial 00 before the numbers given below.

Alain Ducasse's website: www.alain-ducasse.com

La Maison de Sophie

14950 Saint-Etienne La Thillaye, France

Tel: 33-2-31-65-69-97- www.lamaisondesophie.com

Food and Specialty Ingredients

For silky fromage blanc, fine crème fraîche, cultured butter, and cheese accouterments:

Vermont Butter and Cheese Company

Websterville, VT 05678

Tel: 800-884-6287 - www.butterandcheese.net

For excellent domestic foie gras (raw or cooked), fresh ducks, rabbit, squab and guinea hens; pâtés
and mousses; duck confit; cured and smoked meat; truffles and truffle products; chicken, pork, and
game sausages; and many other products:

D'Artagnan

280 Wilson Avenue - Newark, NJ 07105

Tel: 800-327-8246 - www.dartagnan.com

For superb cheeses from around the world, cut to order before shipping:

Ideal Cheese Shop

942 First Avenue (at 52nd Street) - New York, NY 10022

Tel: 800-382-01-09 - www.idealcheese.com

For lovely, bittersweet chocolate dessert cups and cordial cups, as well as specialized baking
chocolates, golden coarse-grained baking sugar, white fondant icing sugar, decorative pastel sugars,
imported yeasts and flours, French fleur de sel from Guérande, and more:

La Cuisine

323 Cameron Street - Alexandria, VA 22314

Tel: 800-521-1176 - www.lacuisineus.com

The following purveyors offer a wide variety of specialty ingredients, including fine olive oils, grapeseed oils, pumpkin seed oils, and more; aged balsamic, sherry, and other vinegars; dried herbs; French mustards; Valrhona bulk chocolate; cocoa powder; imported Italian hand-made pastas; Carnaroli rice, perfect for risottos; imported black pepper; fleur de sel (coarse sea salt) from Brittany; and much more.

Dean and Deluca

Fourteen retail stores in New York City, California, Kansas, North Carolina, and Washington, DC

Tel: 800-221-7714 - www.deandeluca.com

Joie de Vivre

5783 Jerusalem Court, Suite #8 - Modesto, CA 95353

Tel: 800-648-8854 - www.frenchselections.com

Kitchenware

The following kitchenware suppliers offer a panoply of kitchen cookware and baking equipment, including food processors, skillets, baking dishes, silicone muffin cups and baking mats, deep fryers, double-boilers, fish-poachers, electric mixers, Dutch ovens, roasting pans, stock pots, omelette pans, oven thermometers and instant-read digital thermometers, cheese graters, whisks, and Benriner Japanese mandoline slicers used by many chefs, all available by mail order.

Bridge Kitchenware Corporation

711 Third Avenue (at 45th Street) - New York, NY 10017

Tel: 212-688-4220 - www.bridgekitchenware.com

Williams-Sonoma

Stores throughout the U.S.

Tel: 877-812-6235 - www.williams-sonoma.com

King Arthur Flour Baker's Catalogue

The Baker's Store

135 Route 5 South - Norwich, VT 05055

Tel: 800-827-6836 - www.kingarthurflour.com

A NOTE OF THANKS

We gratefully acknowledge the kind participation of the following companies
who graciously and generously supplied their products for photography:

A.TURPAULT, ALESSI, BACCARAT, BERNARDAUD, BODUM, BOUTIQUE SCANDINAVE, CHRISTOFLE, COQUET, FRÉDÉRIQUE
DELBOS, DESHOULIÈRES, DESIGNER'S GUILD, LE CREUSET, NOBILIS, NOËL, REVOL, SCIECLE,
THE CONRAN SHOP, VILLEROY ET BOCH

Photography: Françoise Nicol
Food Styling: Catherine Madani
Proofing: Élisa Vergne
Graphic Design: Anne Chaponnay and Michèle Andrault
Editorial Directors: Hélène Picaud and Emmanuel Jirou-Najou
Photo engraving: Maury Imprimeur

Les Éditions Alain Ducasse

84, avenue Victor Cresson

92 130 Issy-Les-Moulineaux, France

T: +33 (0)1 58 00 21 94   F: +33 (0)1 58 00 21 82

lecedition@wanadoo.fr

www.cookboutic.fr

Distributed in North America by

Stewart, Tabori & Chang

An imprint of Harry N. Abrams, Inc.

115 West 18th Street

New York, NY 10011

www.stcbooks.com

Printed by Worzalla (USA)

Legal deposit: March 2008

ISBN : 978-2-84844-042-2